D0205654

Professional Praise For Cain & So What, Next Pitch!

*"**So What, Next Pitch!** is what the mental game of baseball is all about. Your ability as a player, coach and team to get to the next pitch will make a huge difference in your ability to be successful. **So What, Next Pitch!** is not just a baseball book, this is a book about life. Moving on to the next thing, focusing on what you can control and choosing your response to any given situation will help you in life. That is what attracted me to Brian Cain and that is why we used his program when I was an assistant at Vanderbilt and now as the Head Coach at The University of Maryland. The ideas in this book are game changing and life changing."*

–Eric Bakich, Head Baseball Coach,
The University of Maryland

*"Cain has worked with us at Ole Miss for a number of years and was a key part of our 2009 SEC Championship. His systematic approach to teaching the mental aspects of the game and of life have made a big difference for our program. His ability to make the mental game simple and applicable is what separates him from others in the field. In this book, you learn the system he shares with the top programs in the country to better play one pitch at a time and the **So What, Next Pitch!** mentality is a big part of that process."*

–Mike Bianco, Head Baseball Coach,
The University of Mississippi
2009 Southeastern Conference Champions

*"**So What, Next Pitch!** gives you tips on the mental game of baseball and the quest to be the best player and best person you can be. This book will help you to play at your best when it means the most."*

–Ty Harrington, Head Baseball Coach,
Texas State University

*"**So What, Next Pitch!**. What a great title for a book. This is not a baseball book. This is a book on success and on how to live your life."*
–Donald Hawes, Head Baseball Coach,
Bear River High School, Utah

"Moving on to the next pitch is easier said than done. This book will show you how to do it."
–Gary Gilmore, Head Baseball Coach,
Coastal Carolina University
2012 Big South Conference Champions &
2012 Big South Coach of The Year

*"We have used Cain's mental conditioning system and the **So What, Next Pitch!** mentality at TCU since 2006 and it has been a huge benefit to our program. The information contained in these pages will help to unlock your potential and give you the right perspective to play this game. Baseball is a game of failure. Learning to move on to the next pitch will be a difference maker in your career."*
–Jim Schlossnagle, Head Baseball Coach,
Texas Christian University

"Cain has a way of getting you to challenge your thinking and challenge how you do things. The people he interviewed in this book are some of the most successful in the field of coaching. It should be required reading for anyone who is in the pursuit of excellence regardless of your field of endeavor."
–Todd Whitting, Head Baseball Coach,
The University of Houston

"Cain was a graduate student assistant at Cal State Fullerton in 2002-2003 and he established himself as a hard worker who was only going to have success. In this book, **So What, Next Pitch!**, he has outlined what it takes to be a champion of the mental game and what it takes to play this game between the ears at the highest level. All of our players at Cal State Fullerton will read it, and more importantly, will work to put the concepts into daily practice."

–*Rick Vanderhook, Head Baseball Coach, Cal State Fullerton*
2012 Big West Conference Champions
& 2012 Big West Coach of The Year

"Brian Cain has an energy and an enthusiasm that is contagious. His progressive thinking when it comes to the mental game of baseball has helped him to be an industry-leader in our field and has helped take the mental game of baseball to another level of understanding and application."

–*Steve Trimper, Head Baseball Coach,*
The University of Maine

"We used a lot of what Cain has outlined in this book on our run from 15-16 to the NCAA National Championship in 2004. Cain gives you insight into what **So What, Next Pitch!** is all about. If you are looking to take your game to the next level, this book should be on the top of your reading list."

–*George Horton, Head Baseball Coach,*
The University of Oregon
Head Baseball Coach, Cal State Fullerton,
2004 NCAA National Champions

So What, Next Pitch!

How To Play Your Best When It Means The Most

BRIAN M. CAIN, MS, CMAA

Brian Cain Peak Performance, LLC

***Visit www.SoWhatNextPitch.com/EXTRAS
For BONUS Mental Conditioning Material &
FREE Peak Performance Training Tools***

www.briancain.com
www.briancaininnercircle.com
www.mentalconditioningmanual.com
www.toiletsbricksfishhooksandpride.com

Peak Performance Publishing

Brian M. Cain, MS, CMAA
Peak Performance Coach
Peak Performance Publishing
Brian Cain Peak Performance, LLC

So What, Next Pitch!
How To Play Your Best When It Means The Most
A Masters of the Mental Game Series Book

Printed in United States of America
Edited by Tom Simon, Josh Sorge & Jackson Penfield-Cyr
Cover design & book layout: David Brizendine
Illustrations: Greg Pajala & Nicole Ludwig
Photography: Don Whipple & Paul Lamontangue
Publisher's Catalog-in-Publication
(provided by Quality Books, Inc.)

Brian M. Cain, MS, CMAA
So What, Next Pitch!:
How To Play Your Best When It Means The Most
A Masters of the Mental Game Series Book
Brian M. Cain, MS, CMAA

Library of Congress Control Number: 2012911432
ISBN: 978-0-9830379-2-7

Preface

So What, Next Pitch! – How To Play Your Best When It Means The Most is the second book in the *Masters of the Mental Game Series*. This book is a compilation of articles and interviews from coaches and athletes that expose the significance of the mental game. The author intends for the chapters in this book to be read independently. This allows for the reader's cumulative realization that, through the different experiences of many coaches and athletes, each chapter highlights the recurring lessons and themes of the mental game.

The success stories featured in this book contain information unique to the coach, athlete, or program being highlighted, but the fundamental principles of performance remain the same throughout. This is not a baseball book, this is a book on sport and life with baseball examples. You can use the information in this book to give yourself the best chance for success in anything that you are doing. Success principles are universal. Accepting adversity is a part of life and quickly moving on to the next pitch is something that separates the good from the great.

This is a book for people looking for simple yet extremely effective ways to improve their performance. This book will not go into theory or research, but is itself a body of research in which you are able to hear from the best coaches in the country on what works and how they run various aspects of their mental conditioning programs.

So What, Next Pitch! is about what has worked for real people in real programs. Whether you are a veteran of the mental game or just getting started, this book will provide insight and information you can use to help unlock your potential and perform at your best when it means the most.

Here is to your success in the quest to dominate the day and move on from the last pitch to the next one, to living in the moment and not counting the days, but making the days count. Remember that the destination is the disease and the journey is the reward. Enjoy the process and live *So What, Next Pitch!*

Dedication

This book is dedicated to all of the great coaches and athletes out there that have allowed me to work with them and their programs and have given me an opportunity to teach the mental game.

To Tom Simon for showing me how to be an adult but keep baseball a kids game. Thank you for your leadership, wisdom and friendship over the years.

To my father Joe Cain for the countless hours he spent in the back yard teaching me how to throw, catch and hit. Without those important life skills in my arsenal, who knows what I would be doing.

ACKNOWLEDGMENTS

It is with sincere and deep appreciation that I acknowledge the support and guidance of the following people who helped make this book possible.

One big Power Clap to Ken Ravizza, Mark Scalf, Randy Hood, Scott Jackson, Philip O'Neal, Ron Wolforth, Dan Gable, Brian Mitchell, Jack Dahm, Ryan Brownlee, Casey O'Rourke, Harvey Dorfman, Eric Degre, Justin Dehmer, Bill Currier, Steve Trimper, Dave Serrano, Glenn Swanson, Johnny "Moonlight" Graham, Cody Cipriano, Jim Schlossnagle, George Horton, Hunter Yurachek, Mike Coutts, Patrick Murphy, Bob Tewksbury, Don Whipple, Paul Lamontangue, Greg Pajala, Jeff Davis, David Brizendine, Peter Scott, Doris Bruey, Tom Simon, Josh Sorge, Jackson Penfield-Cyr, and Meghan Turcot for their contributions to this book.

I would also like to acknowledge the many coaches and athletes that have blessed me with the opportunity to work with you on mastering the mental game. There are too many of you to mention.

If you are upset that your name is not mentioned here as some of you were when **Toilets, Bricks, Fish Hooks and PRIDE** came out, remember, check your ego, life is not about you! It's about the young people you teach, living your life to the fullest, loving the people you lead, learning as if you would live forever, laughing at yourself and leaving a legacy of greatness that this World was a better place because you were here, not because you are gone.

If you are reading this book, it is my goal that you are equipped with some tools to leave this world a better place than you found it.

Contents

129

FOREWORD

Baseball is a tough game played by tough competitors. To be successful you must learn to embrace adversity and handle the failure that is built into this great game. The funny thing is—the game of baseball mirrors the game of life. It is all about moving onto the next pitch and playing/living for the moment while still having a plan as to how you will go about giving yourself the best chance to get the desired end result.

The 2007 UC Irvine Baseball team had a storybook season to those on the outside; but on the inside, our season was full of adversity and challenge. We embraced that adversity and capped that season with the greatest run in program history going from the unknown to the pinnacle of college baseball—the Men's College World Series in Omaha.

In *So What, Next Pitch!*, Brian Cain gives you great insight into what champions know that most people don't. That failure is an unavoidable part of the game and of life. Failure will make you bitter or it will make you better. You will get discouraged and run away or you will get encouraged and run towards your goal and meet your opponent head on.

If you are going to give yourself the best chance for success you will pay close attention to what the people interviewed in this book are saying. Many people make the mistake in thinking that you are either born mentally tough or you are not. To not have the skill of mental toughness is an excuse. Mental toughness is a decision you make every day when you get out of bed. Mental toughness is a lifestyle, not an event.

We started using Brian Cain with our program at UC Irvine in 2006 and I had previously worked with him at Cal State Fullerton in 2002 and 2003. His system and program will speed up your learning curve and help you play your best when it means the most.

Can you be mentally tough without this book. Yes. Will you increase your chances for success if you read this book and then live the principles being taught. Absolutely.

Success is a choice. So is failure. If you want to be successful on the field and want to be successful in life having the right perspective, attitude and mental approach will separate you from the competition. Most athletic competitions and competitions in life are won or lost before they even start. Give yourself the best chance for success by working at your mental game.

Dave Serrano
Head Baseball Coach
The University of Tennessee
2010 & 2011 Big West Conference Coach of The Year
2008, 2010, 2011 Big West Conference Champions
2010 Team USA Baseball Pitching Coach
2010 Big West Conference Coach of The Year
2009 NCAA College World Series, Cal State Fullerton
2007 Baseball America National Coach of The Year
2007 NCAA College World Series, UC Irvine
2004 NCAA National Champions, Asst. Coach, Cal State Fullerton
1 of 11 Coaches To Lead Two Programs To NCAA College World Series

INTRODUCTION

Physical strength and conditioning has been widely accepted by coaches and athletes for years. Mental conditioning, training the right thought process, perspective, attitude and will, is now becoming a staple in athletic development from the little league to the big leagues.

I have worked as a metal conditioning coach for the Washington Nationals organization, with teams at the Men's College World Series in Omaha and at the Women's College World Series in Oklahoma City, and with numerous top collegiate and high school baseball and softball programs. This book contains many of those experiences so that you can accelerate the learning curve and start to master the mental game.

The coaches and athletes interviewed for this book have graciously shared their experiences and I am confident that you will benefit greatly from their wisdom. In life, I have found that there is no substitute for experience. I have also learned that there are two types of experience: expensive and inexpensive.

Expensive experience is what you gain from your own trials and errors, from your own performances. Inexpensive experience is what you learn from others who have been where you are and where you want to go. This book is loaded with inexpensive experience for the coach, athlete, athletic director or performer in life looking to be at their best when it means the most.

For the athletes reading this book, attack each day with

a zeal for life and a passion that today might very well be your last day to play your sport. That may be cliché, but it is the best way I have learned to make your dreams become a reality and make the impossible possible.

For the coach reading this book, realize the importance of the third word in this sentence. Coach. In my opinion, coach is one of the most powerful words in the world. For someone to call you coach means you have an opportunity to have tremendous positive, and unfortunately, negative impact on that person's life.

We have all played for and been around those coaches who were confidence-cutters and energy-takes. In this book, you will learn how you can maximize your performance and teach life skills through sport to the athletes you lead by challenging your and their perspective.

Mental toughness, the ability to learn from failure, to say "So What, Next Pitch!" in the face of adversity, is a skill that you teach. Some athletes will come into your program without mental toughness, that is the fault of them, their parents, and previous coaches; but if they leave your program without mental toughness, that is YOUR fault.

For the non-coach or athlete reading this book, my hat's off to you for picking up what might look like a baseball book, but is truly a book on the psychology of successful living and elite performance. I challenge you to pursue your dreams, make the impossible possible and live your life to the fullest. Anyone who tells you that you can't do something is projecting their limited self-belief on you. Flush It! Everyone thought that winning 88 straight baseball games was impossible until Justin Dehmer did it at Martensdale-St. Mary's in Iowa. If they can do that, what can you do?

Every individual truly has limitless potential. I am confident that this book will help you to turn that potential power in to production power and help you start to perform at your best when it means the most, each and every day! TODAY!!!

Enjoy your journey to becoming a Master of the Mental Game. I guarantee you it will be worth your while.

PART 1

Interviews with
Masters of The Mental Game

Chapter 1 | A HISTORIC HIGH SCHOOL WINNING STREAK

Coach Shares Mental Strategies Used During Nation's Longest Winning Streak

This interview is between Brian Cain and Justin Dehmer, the head baseball coach at Martensdale-St. Mary's High School in Iowa. At the time of the interview Coach Dehmer and his team were riding an eighty game (80) winning streak. Since the time of this interview, the team ran their record to an all-time high school baseball record of 87 games with the conclusion of the 2011 season. Portsmouth, NH High School, who plays baseball in the spring, surpassed Martensdale-St. Mary's record and ran the new National High School Baseball Consecutive Wins Record to 89. Martensdale-St. Mary's plays their baseball in the summer and came up just short of tying the record at game 89.

Coach Dehmer leads his team by emphasizing an intent and unified team focus. This focus is not on furthering the team's winning streak, nor on the national record. The team is not focused on its second-straight state championship. Rather, Coach Dehmer has his team focused on playing the game one pitch at a time.

COACH DEHMER BACKGROUND

BC: Could you give a little bit of your background into how you got to where you are today as the Martensdale-St. Mary's head coach?

JD: I'm from Phoenix, Arizona. I grew up playing high-school baseball at a big 5-A school there, went on to Central Arizona where my head coach was Clint Myers, who is now the head women's softball coach at Arizona State. Coach Myers and the Sun Devils have had great success and have won National Championships in 2008 and 2011. I went from Central Arizona to Kansas State University and played there for one year. During that year I broke my finger.

I ended up getting a medical redshirt for that whole season, went back to Arizona for two years where I finished up at Grand Canyon University, got my teaching degree, and got a chance to play a couple more years of baseball and finish off my career.

Then my wife, whom I met at Kansas State, and I decided to move back to Iowa, start a family, and put down some roots, and that's how I ended up in the great state of Iowa. My wife and her family are from Iowa and we just thought this would be a great place to raise a family.

I was teaching at a place called Oelwein High School, a small 1-A school, as the junior varsity and assistant varsity coach for a couple of years and had some success. Then Martensdale-St. Mary's had a job opening, which I took knowing they great tradition, a lot of state tournament appearances; one of those places where baseball is in the culture and taken very seriously.

My first two years as head coach we were 19-11 (2008) and then 25-11 (2009). Then in 2010 we went 43-0, and right now (2011), we are currently 37-0.

ABOUT MARTENSDALE-ST. MARY'S

BC: Talk a little bit about St. Mary's. When some coaches see the title "St. Mary's," they will immediately think that it's a school with religious affiliation, and maybe a school that can recruit because it's a small private school. Is that the case?

JD: It's a public school. St. Mary's is a tiny, tiny town. If you drive through it and blink, you're going to miss it. The first thing you see when you come into St. Mary's is the baseball field and a gym in the outfield that's our indoor facility with some batting cages.

The school itself happens to be in Martensdale, but the baseball field is in St. Mary's. The two towns joined up; it happens a lot here in Iowa where you have towns combining to have a school and a school district. A lot of people look at our school name and think we're a private school. We are public. In 2010 we played St. Mary's Remsen in the championship game, which happened to be a private school, so there was a big confusion there amongst everybody thinking that we both were private schools playing for the public-school state title.

BC: How many students attend your school?

JD: I think the senior class this year was forty-two or forty-five. It's a small school, 1-A is as small as you can get in Iowa, and that is small. We are not real large but have a lot of good baseball tradition. Some families have moved into our district, and we take some heat for that, but when you do things right and are successful, people want to be a part of what you're doing.

SUCCESSFUL HIGH SCHOOL COACHES GET RECRUITING RAP

BC: I see a lot of successful high-school coaches getting that label of being recruiters, but high-school kids and parents aren't idiots *(well... some of them are)*. They want their kid to play at the next level. They're going to move into the town so they can go to the school that has the best coach and the best system for development and does things the right way. There are a lot of coaches out there who do things right and get the recruiting card played on them.

You've established Martensdale-St. Mary's as a program that's doing great things for people who have a passion for baseball. It sounds like people who want to have a great experience can't pay to come to your school, but they can move into your district and be a part of that.

JD: Correct. I tell kids the story about when we went to the Junior College World Series at Central Arizona. Every single guy on our team went on to play at a four-year school. Some of those guys got only one inning of pitching experience that year. They still went on to play somewhere, and that's kind of how we phrase it, too: If we have success as a team, then you as an individual are going to get looks, and you're probably going to get an opportunity to play at the next level. Three of our four seniors went on to play last year, and we have only two seniors this year and they're definitely going to go somewhere. We've built a place where kids can come in and get better for four years and go on and play somewhere else.

THE SYSTEM FOR SUCCESS

BC: Talk a little bit about your system. More exciting than the winning streak to me is the way you've done it. Can you talk about your process from a mental-game standpoint, where you got your system of teaching the mental game, and some of the things you brought to Martensdale-St. Mary's?

JD: In my playing experience, I was definitely NOT a master of the mental game in any way, shape, or form. I was probably one of the worst. I would beat myself up after a bad performance to no end. When I became a coach, something I was going to have to be really, really good at was teaching kids how to manage their heads, and making sure they give themselves the best chance to succeed on a consistent basis. I was a very inconsistent player, always up-and-down. One night I'd be hot and the next I'd be 0-for-4.

I had a pretty good grasp of the X's and O's and how to treat kids, but I wanted to grab onto something that was worthwhile and made sense to me. A lot of what you use in the mental game, and all of your terminology, like the "mental bricks," it just stuck with me and it clicked. I was just amazed. I couldn't get enough of it and just kept feeding it to our kids.

Our big thing was the Five P's of Peak Performance, which is to live in the Present moment, focus on the Process, stay Positive, have a champion's Perspective, and Prepare to the best of your ability. We try to play the game the way it's supposed to be played, which is pitch-by-pitch.

It sounds simple but getting kids to actually understand it and to have a routine and a process to go through of getting a deep breath, refocusing on some sort of focal point, and getting back into the present takes time to develop. The mental game is something that they have to practice and work on. We make them write down their routine and what they are going to do to prepare and when the adversity hits so that we all know ahead of time. I can almost tell you when guys are going to get a hit when they get into the box. I can tell when guys are locked in when I see them take that big deep breath and get in the present moment.

We also work a lot on our players' perspective. We try to teach our players that baseball is just a game, this is not life or death; there's a lot bigger things out there and more important things than this game, and we're just going to enjoy it now and stay positive.

We also emphasize being a good teammate and sticking with a focus on the process over the outcome. That has been huge for us. We keep statistics, but statistics aren't important to me or the team. The most important things are things what we call quality pitches and quality at-bats. We keep track of those on a player-by-player basis. If the hitter moves a runner up with no outs, then that's a quality at-bat. There's nothing wrong with that, that's helping the team succeed, instead of an 0-for-1 that's a 1-for-1 in that kid's mind. He did his job. He moved the runner over, now we have a chance to score a run. The process is something that we really hammer home. It's all about committing to what we do on a daily basis and having quality practices.

We've had some great success with this approach. Our varsity has been amazing, but in the four years I've been there our JV has lost only five games. There is a definite trickle-down effect. Our JV players are doing the same thing our varsity kids are doing, and when it's their turn to step in it's a comfort factor and they know exactly what's going on.

Quality practice and quality preparation is a big one for us. I have to say we run some pretty long practices, but we run some pretty good ones, and we put a lot of time into preparing them. I think that's one of the biggest reasons why we have been successful; our players are getting better all the time.

ESTABLISHING A PROGRAM GRADES 9-12

BC: You talked about getting your JV and varsity players together, how much of practice is spent together with JV and varsity?

JD: We're a small school. This year we have big numbers: we have twenty-eight kids between the JV and varsity, but in years past we were right around twenty. Our JV team practices with our varsity, so they're really getting four years of the same coaching. When they come in as freshmen we use the same terminology and language for four years. Flushing the mental bricks, playing it one pitch at a time; they hear it daily for four years. That is really one of the reasons I enjoy coaching at a small school.

Where you coach at a bigger, 4-A program, you don't get to see those kids for all four years. You hope your other coaches are doing the same thing, but that's not always a guarantee. I know what's going on with my JV and even our seventh- and eighth-grade teams. They're doing the same stuff we are, so it's all the way through our program. It's a huge part of our culture and our success.

PRACTICE PHILOSOPHY

BC: Let's shift gears here for a bit. Can you talk about your practice philosophy? I think a lot of coaches think "okay, right now we're working on the mental game and then we're going to work on the physical game." Do you see working on the mental and physical game as something that you do together or are they separate?

JD: I see them as one and the same. When we're allowed to practice with our pitchers and catchers before practice officially starts in May, we'll start mentioning the mental game to them then.

We'll have a ten- or fifteen-minute session when we're breaking down the mental game and reviewing things they have read or seen in videos. Once we start practice and we're on the field in a live situation, coaching the mental game is more of an on-the-fly thing, where guys will turn to each other and say, "Hey, flush it, man." They literally will say that to each other during practices and games, and they'll get each other back on the same page, playing with a "So What, Next Pitch!" mentality.

It's an atmosphere of excellence that we've created and it kind of runs itself, really. There are times when we as coaches will pull guys aside and say, "Hey, we got a lot of game left, let's get rid of that inning. Let's go back out there on the mound next inning and go one pitch at a time and flush it. It wasn't great but we can do better and let's not let that hamper our future here." And it's pretty cool to see how it has all evolved and taken on a life of its own.

PLAYERS MUST TAKE OWNERSHIP

BC: It sounds like the ownership is with the players and their belief in the system is pretty solid.

JD: 100%. We have media coverage around the streak and when our guys get interviewed, I'll watch it on TV and our guys are using the language, saying things like, "Yeah, we just play it one pitch at a time and we're not going to worry about what happened in the past or what's going to happen in the future, we're locked in on today and trying to get better today." It's pretty cool to see guys interviewed and they're saying basically the same thing you've been saying for four years about how we want to approach the game and play it.

We're a physically talented team, but I've always said we want to be better mentally than we are physically, and if we're better mentally than we are physically, then we're going to win a lot more games than we lose. The players have bought into it and they have no doubt that it's the reason for our eighty wins in a row.

We've fought in some pretty close one-run games and come-back games; games when we've really had to play one pitch at a time. We would continue to grind it out and play that way while the other team, maybe for only one inning, takes a lapse, and we turn a walk or one error into two or three runs and all of a sudden we have the momentum, and we're ahead. ***Sticking with the process and playing pitch-to-pitch has been the reason for our success;*** there's no doubt about that.

ONE-PITCH WARRIORS

BC: One of the things that you've talked about in the media is this idea of being a "one-pitch warrior." What is a one-pitch warrior?

JD: A one-pitch warrior is a guy who plays the game one-pitch at a time and knows how to do that when something bad happens. He has the ability to move on to the next pitch. It may not be instantaneously, but he has a routine where he allows himself to take a deep breath, relax, and get back into playing the game one pitch at a time, whether it be fielding the next ground ball, hitting the cutoff, or coming back after the umpire just hosed him on strike two. Being able to still battle and fight and have a chance to take a good quality swing on a good pitch, and give us an opportunity for that ball to find some area out there where it can impact the game.

Our guys are really good at handling adversity. We played a 3-A school that was a good-quality, state-tournament type of team and had been there quite a few times, and their coach came up to us after the game and said, "I was really impressed with your guys; I've never seen you play before but I'm really impressed with how your guys handled themselves. They just never quit." We were down 5-2 going into the fourth inning and we battled back and scored six unanswered runs and won, 8-5. I saw that as a testament to our guys and how they go about being one-pitch warriors.

ROUTINES IMPORTANT PART OF PROGRAM

BC: Talk about the routine at the plate and on the mound of the one-pitch warrior, and the importance of breathing in the routine.

JD: It's something we talk about from the first practice throughout the season. I can really almost tell you when a guy is going to hit the ball hard on our team. That's how well I know our guys' routines and how diligent they go about taking that deep breath. Every guy's got a different way of doing it but there's some sort of deep breath involved on a focal point. They all do it and it helps them to "slow the game down."

We practice fast so we can slow it down. We never want to let the game speed up on us, we want it to speed up on our opponent. We want to play it one pitch at a time, use our routines every pitch, whether we're in the field, on the mound, or in the batter's box. The routine gets our guys locked into where they need to be when they need to be there.

That's a key phrase for us as well, "lock it in." Lock it in means to get that routine going and get back to your plan. One pitch at a time, be a one-pitch warrior, and let's see what happens with the results, because we can never control the results, only our actions.

MENTAL IMAGERY IN PRACTICE

BC: What about mental imagery? Is that something you guys use at all? Do you as a coach use it with them to prepare or do you ask them to use it in practice or in games?

JD: At the beginning of the year I thought that was one of the things we were lacking, so I told them, as soon as we started with winter workouts, that I'd challenge our guys to go through just five minutes a day, if they could, before the season started, and look at plays they need to make and how they want to swing the bat and make pitches. I wanted them to visualize going through the whole process, the routine of what they're going to do before they get in the box.

I also said, "Let's not just think about driving a ball out of the ballpark or off the fence or making a great diving play, let's also visualize what you're going to do after you just threw a ball away." How you respond to adversity is more important to me than making a great play or hitting the double. Handling adversity is going to take you a long way because every one of us is going to get a bad call. Every one of us is going to have a strikeout in a game or make an error. The most important thing is how we handle it. What are we going to do to let it go and get to the next pitch?

I challenge them to go through their release and know what they are going to do after those things happen. Going through their release is important and we feel that it helps us win games.

Our offensive philosophy is **BASE2**, where we want to have Big innings, we want to Answer back, we want to Score first, we want to Extend the lead, and we want to score with two outs. Defensively, we want to avoid those same things. So far this season, in thirty-seven games, we have given up only six unearned runs, our defense has been awesome. Part of that is learning to focus on what we can control and what we need to do to be successful, *our defensive routine of stepping into our circle of focus and playing it one pitch at a time.*

THE STREAK

BC: Let's talk about the streak. A lot of times success will breed complacency. In a game like baseball, where the best team never wins, it's always the team that plays the best, how have you been able to maintain that level of performance over two years and eighty games?

JD: We have an extremely talented team. Last year we led the state, not just in our class but the entire state, in almost every offensive category, and then to top it off we also had the most shutouts, the most strikeouts, pitching-wise. We weren't a one-dimensional team and we aren't this year, either. We're second in home runs and we're still leading the state in strikeouts, so we have an enormous amount of talent and a very deep pitching staff, which at the 1-A level is pretty uncommon. If you've got one really good guy you've got a chance, but we've got probably three or four guys who are really, really good and would be number ones in just about everyone else's program, and we've got other guys who could pick up innings for us on the mound.

That physical talent is part of it, but at some point you figure you're going to get beat by somebody because you take an off night or run into a good pitcher. Our guys have just stuck with the process. I'm trying to get them ready for every game the best I can and not having an off night, I think it's a testament to how we go about our batting practice and what we do pre-game because we don't really practice all that much once the season starts.

We have an hour before our game and then we get on the bus, or we have an hour before our home game, and that's our practice really. So that's when we have to get our ground balls and our fly balls in and do all of our work in the cages to get ready. We have a lot of guys who are extremely competitive. We have a two-time state wrestling champion who will probably win his third this year as a senior. He went undefeated as a junior, and his winner's mentality is contagious on our team. You talk about a streak, he's the one with the longest streak on our team: he hasn't lost in wrestling or in baseball for two years.

We have guys who just love to win and love to compete. They have also truly bought into the mental-game philosophy that you helped bring to the table for us and I tried to implement in our program. I think the combination of the two has been our success formula.

ADVICE FOR COACHES – BE DETAIL ORIENTED

BC: If you had to offer a bit of advice to high school and college coaches around the country, something that you have done that has been successful, what would that one thing be?

JD: Be detail-oriented in everything you do. Whether it be the way we take batting practice or how we chart our guys during the game, I try to break it down into a science and get as much information as I can during the process.

We put emphasis on quality at-bats and bunting, and that's part of our process. If we do that during practice I think we're going to do it during the game. If we put pressure on them through competition in practice that translates into a more competitive team come game time.

Make practice as game-like as possible, and in the games focus on the process, never the outcome. We're charting quality at-bats, we're charting balls and strikes for our pitchers and quality innings. When you have a system that you can present to your team that you believe in, it's going to rub off on your players.

Players are going to find success through the process and when they can stay positive and embrace adversity good things are going to happen. It's about creating a system that will run itself, whether you are there as the coach or not. We've been pretty fortunate with the guys we have, but our system is more important than any of us. We've got a whole other JV team that's doing the same thing and it's the system that wins games for us, not necessarily our players, on a nightly basis.

SYSTEMS = SUCCESS

BC: Establishing a system of excellence and a right and wrong way to do things, from the way you stand for the National Anthem to the way you take batting practice to the way you clean up the dugout after games, is essential to achieving excellence. Having systems for all those little things makes it so there are no little things, which makes success happen more consistently.

JD: Exactly. I think we found a system that works and we're always trying to find better ways to improve it and things to implement that we think will work better. As of now what we're doing seems to be working pretty well. The system has got to be there, there's no doubt about that. You can't have kids who don't know what's going on out there. As you said, establishing a system of excellence will lead you there.

CONTACT COACH DEHMER

For more information about Coach Dehmer please visit his web site www.1pitchwarrior.com or e-mail him directly at jdehmer@gmail.com for his availability to work with teams on the mental game.

KEY POINTS FOR REVIEW:

The Five P's of Peak Performance:

> **(1) live in the Present;**
>
> **(2) focus on the Process;**
>
> **(3) stay Positive;**
>
> **(4) have a champion's Perspective; and**
>
> **(5) Prepare to the best of your ability.**

- **A one-pitch warrior is a player who plays the game one pitch at a time even in the face of adversity.**

- **Focusing on a focal point and taking a deep breath is a way of slowing the game down.**

- **Great coaches have systems within their program that are repeatable and can be implemented at any level of their program.**

- **"Lock It In" means getting back to your routine.**

- **A system of excellence gives you the best chance to yield excellent results.**

> *Visit www.SoWhatNextPitch.com/EXTRAS*
> *For BONUS Mental Conditioning Material &*
> *FREE Peak Performance Training Tools*

Chapter 2 | NATIONAL CHAMPIONSHIP
MENTAL CONDITIONING

Alabama's Patrick Murphy

Shares Essentials of Tide's Mental-Conditioning Program

BC: Coach Murphy, you're one of the most successful softball coaches in the country and led The University of Alabama Softball Program to the 2012 NCAA National Championship. If I were to ask you to talk about mental conditioning for the game of softball, what sort of things would you talk about?

PM: Softball is definitely a mental game. If the athlete feels good about herself, it's definitely going to carry over into the softball performance side of it. If she's not feeling good about herself, it's definitely going to negatively affect her on the field as well. *I think the mental game is a huge part of our game with female athletes.*

BC: Are there things that you do as the coach to try to make the players feel good before the game?

PM: We talk about past performances or practices that week if somebody did really well or will look at pre-game batting practice. I've changed lineups ten minutes before the game, when somebody has had a great batting practice, and I'll go up to her individually and say, "You know, you deserve to start, you were awesome today."

More times than not they've rewarded us with great performances. Batting practice carries over to the game in softball a lot I think. Sometimes it's a gut feeling, but most of the time if they look good, you can tell that they feel good about where they are at that day and how they are playing, and then chances are they're going to play well in the game.

SIGNS OF SUCCESS

BC: If I were to ask about coaching the mental game, what are some of the things you would talk about? You have the "Process over Outcome" and "Get Big" signs in the dugout and the "Two Outs, So What?" sign on the foul pole. What are some of the things you do that you consider coaching the mental game?

PM: *The signs serve as great reminders for us, they're great visual cues of the thought processes that we want to have. We do a lot of daily reminders about the process.* I probably talk at least three times a practice about putting a good swing on the ball, and if the outfielder makes a diving catch, that's a great at-bat, it's a great swing, and take confidence from that. Feel good about it because you crushed it.

In the weight room, we talk about the mental game all the time. Conditioning is a chance to improve mental toughness and when you have a hard workout or a run and you might not feel like you want to do it, or you can't do it, that's a great time to practice your mental game and *act differently than how you feel.*

We're in the weight room three times a week all year so it's a great time to utilize the mental skills we want on the field. *Whenever I read anything about a similar situation of an athlete, I clip out the article and send it to whomever I think it mirrors on my team.*

SHARING OF ARTICLES A SUCCESS

BC: Can you think of one specific example that you've used with an article or share a story that you felt has made a difference?

PM: After the Texas Christian University team played so well in the baseball 2010 College World Series, I was researching them on the internet and there was an article about their captain and catcher, Bryan Holiday, that was all about his journey of becoming, behind the scenes, a starter and then all of a sudden he is the guy holding everybody accountable. It was perfect for one of our seniors this year.

Holiday talked about how he had to hold a teammate accountable and it was uncomfortable for him but he made the choice that he would rather win than not, and he would rather be respected than liked. I think that's a lot tougher for female athletes to do than male athletes because they're extremely worried about whether people like them.

BC: Some of the best leaders that you've had, have they fallen into that category of rather being respected than liked?

PM: Definitely. We had one in our first four years in the program. We had no business of playing in a regional final in our fourth year, and I think it was largely due to this one player. Christy Kyle was one of the best leaders we've ever had.

CHARACTERISTICS OF A GREAT LEADER

BC: What were some of the characteristics that made her a great leader?

PM: She was tougher on herself than anyone else. ***She held herself to a higher standard of excellence.*** She was one of the first players I had coached who walked the walked so she could talk the talk. She was not afraid to get into people's faces and it was very much her policing the team herself.

I can remember several articles written about Pat Summit and the University of Tennessee women's basketball program that said you know you have a successful program when the players themselves police their fellow teammates. When we started doing that I felt like we were going to be successful.

CORE COVENANTS ARE KEY

BC: Shift gears here a little bit and talk about the core covenants of Alabama Softball. You have had these as the foundation of your program for years. What is the purpose of your program's core covenants and what difference have they made in the program?

PM: *What our core covenants provide is a systematic way of saying, we want the whole package, we don't want just a winning softball team; we want good citizens, good students, good teammates, people who will give back to the community, and all the things that go into being a good human being. That is how we want to do things and we want them to s*tart living those values as early as possible.

We want them to realize that there's life after softball. That's one of the hardest things; unlike baseball, there are not many opportunities after college for playing the game, and we've got to get them prepared for that sudden moment when it's over.

A lot of our core covenants help them with getting out in the community and doing internships with their majors and realizing that every time they shake a hand it's a six-second job interview.

BC: So the core covenants really are not just going to help them win games in softball, but they're going to help them win in life?

PM: Definitely. I think the process opens their eyes a little bit; they know that this is a four-year gig, that's it. *It's our job as coaches to use these four years to prepare them for a long and successful life after softball.* Their four years at the University of Alabama go by extremely fast and we want to make sure they take advantage of all the opportunities presented to them. They need to realize that they're not going to be a celebrity for the rest of their life as they may be here for four years and there are a lot of things that go into preparing them for the real world, a lot of the things we talk about with the covenants and our mission statement.

FOUNDATIONS OF SUCCESS

BC: You've had a lot of success here at the University of Alabama: Southeastern Conference Championships, College World Series appearances. What would you say is the foundation of your program? If you had to say, "These are the things that have been consistent with every team we've had that has been successful," what would those things be?

PM: *When you surround yourself with good people, good things happen.* We have been blessed to have great assistant coaches, great athletic trainers, managers, strength coaches, and players. I can't think of a negative staff member whom we've had, and that's a rarity. I'm still great friends with one of our first athletic trainers and one of our first student-managers. There is a huge sense of family in our program.

We teach our players that we want people who want to be here. That's our #1 goal in recruiting. Once you're on campus as an Alabama softball player, there's no such thing as divorce in our program, you're here and you're going to be here for four or five years and we're going to figure out a way to make you successful. There are going to be ups and downs and we'll work through them, but once you're here you're stuck with us and we're stuck with you, so we have to commit to making it work.

We've only had one kid who played four years and didn't graduate. You're going to see your teammates more than your own family so we want to get along and definitely want to have fun with what we do.

BC: You said "surround yourself with good people," is there anything else that you feel has been a cornerstone of your success?

PM: I think we *still have an underdog mentality.* I always say we haven't done anything yet until we win a national championship, and we're still the underdog. We're still fighting for respect. Play with a chip on your shoulder. I think if they believe that they've arrived, that is when we will get humbled and are going to get passed by. I think when you consider yourself the underdog, you don't settle, you stay humble and hungry.

BC: Is there anything that I haven't asked you that you think is important, any last nuggets of wisdom?

PM: We had our staff meeting the other day and one of the first things they said is that *we want to look for new and different ways to teach the game. We want to be innovative. We want to be creative. We don't want to be the "same old, same old" again because if you stand still you're going to get passed.* So we're always looking for new and different ways to do things.

However, you must also continue to do the things that you have done that have made you successful. Don't forget those things. It's kind of like Vince Lombardi and the Green Bay Packers. They had five plays and they mastered those five plays and even though everybody knew what was coming, they couldn't stop them.

That mentality translated on the field to "don't forget the fundamentals," but we're also going to look for new ways to teach because I think with today's kids, it's got to be a little bit new and different for them to stick with it because attention spans are not very long.

I still go to as many camps and clinics that I can, both softball and baseball, and sit and listen to learn what other people are doing. It's finding a balance between trying to be new and innovative but also keeping your hands on what has worked.

KEY POINTS FOR REVIEW:

- Act differently than how you feel.

- Signs are great reminders, serving as visual cues for desired thought processes.

- Core covenants provide is a systematic means for teams to commit to the whole package, holding the team focus beyond winning games and toward being good citizens, good students, good teammates and all the things that go into being a good human being.

- It is the coach's duty to utilize the four years with each athlete to prepare them for a long and successful life after sport.

- When you surround yourself with good people, good things happen.

- Keep an underdog mentality.

- Coaches must look for new and different ways to do things. Be innovative. Be creative. Don't settle for the "same old, same old" methods of teaching, because if you stand still you're going to get passed.

- Go to as many camps and clinics as you can. Learn what other people are doing. Improvement is about finding a balance between trying to be new and innovative but also keeping your hands on what has worked.

Chapter 3 | LEADERSHIP IN ATHLETICS

Coastal Carolina Athletic Director
Shares Insight into Developing Leaders

Hunter Yurachek is currently the Director of Athletics at Coastal Carolina University in Conway, South Carolina. Yurachek previously served as the Executive Senior Associate Athletic Director at the University of Akron, the Associate Athletic Director for Marketing at the University of Virginia, the Senior Associate Athletic Director at Western Carolina University, Assistant Athletic Director and Director of Marketing and Promotions at Vanderbilt University, and as the Assistant Director of Marketing and Promotions at Wake Forest University. He has extensive background in external department relations including marketing and promotions, media relations, ticket operations, financial development, video operations, and merchandising.

Yurachek grew up in Charlotte, North Carolina and earned his bachelor's degree in business management at Guilford College, where he was a four-year letter winner for the basketball program. He then received his master's degree in sports administration from the University of Richmond. Yurachek is a member of the National Association of Collegiate Athletic Directors and National Association of Collegiate Marketing Administrators and is very involved in numerous community service activities. He shared his perspective on what the best coaches he has worked with do to separate themselves from others.

COMMITMENT TO THE COMMON GOAL

The best coaches that I have been around in the nearly 20 years I have been involved in intercollegiate athletics are the ones who bring together student-athletes, regardless of cultural and socio-economic backgrounds, and get them to commit to a common goal. For example, in basketball you have twelve to thirteen student-athletes on a team and only five will be on the court at once. A great coach is able to get each student-athlete to buy into his or her role and get everyone to be on the same page and committed to the team goals over those of the individual. Some coaches have that skill; that ability to get people to come together and buy into the common goal. It is a critical skill to possess, especially at the collegiate level.

CARE FOR THE ATHLETES AS PEOPLE FIRST

Another characteristic of great coaches is that they truly care about their student-athletes as individuals. Great coaches care more about their student-athletes' development as people than they do about winning games. They understand that if you develop good people, winning will take care of itself. They genuinely care for the student-athlete as a person first and foremost and will not sacrifice the student-athlete's health or well-being to win a game or get to the next level of the coaching profession.

The best coaches I have been around can tell you what their former players are doing today. They can do this because there is a relationship that was formed, cultivated and nurtured when the student-athletes played for them and they continue to be engaged in the lives of their former student-athletes.

I think that coaches get their student-athletes to buy into one common goal or vision because their athletes know that they care about them as people and have their best interests in mind. We have all heard the cliché "Student-Athletes don't care what you know, until they know that you care" and I think that is true when you talk about getting student-athletes to give up their personal goals for the betterment of the team and for getting athletes to buy into your vision of what the team is all about.

I refer back to my college coach Jack Jensen and from day one the team knew that he cared about each of us. To this day he is one of the most loyal human beings I have ever known. He passed away this summer and I spoke to him a few weeks prior to his passing and at the age of seventy-two, almost twenty-seven years after I had played for him, he still was engaged in my life. I remember being willing to do anything for him as a coach because I knew he cared for me as a person.

UTILIZE THE STRENGTHS OF OTHER PEOPLE

One of the things that coaches can do to help get their athletes to buy into their vision for the program is utilize the resources and people around them and expose their athletes to other successful people and leaders from outside of their team. It could be bringing in a coach from another program on your campus to talk about your core covenants or an element of excellence, such as discipline or selflessness, which is necessary on any successful team.

Our baseball team at Coastal Carolina University had its best season in school history in 2010 when they went undefeated in the conference (25-0), a feat that is nearly impossible in baseball, and the team earned the #4 national seed in the NCAA tournament. They brought in a Peak Performance Coach and he helped to give the coaching staff and players a common language and set of mental skills to help get everyone on the same page.

In this day and age of Facebook, cell phones, text messages and all of the distractions, it can be hard for coaches and athletes to live in the present. They spend a lot of time counting down the days till the next game instead of making each of those days count by working to improve their game or by investing in their teammates and team chemistry.

Using a retreat or having an outsider come in can help you to get the team to contribute to and take ownership of that vision. As the coach, you must first have a vision of where you want to go and then work hard to get the team to become the vision of the athletes, otherwise there will not be the ownership from the players and the buy-in will be diminished. You have to lead them to the vision and get them to agree to that vision. You need to outline what each individual can do on a daily basis to help the team get there and when everyone is doing a little bit each day toward that vision, you will have given your team the best chance to accomplish success.

DEVELOP A RELATIONSHIP OUTSIDE OF ATHLETICS

Letting your players see and know you outside of the competitive arena is critical to them seeing you as a person rather than simply their coach. Having athletes over to your house for a team dinner, doing some kind of community service project or going on a team retreat allows your athletes to see their coach in a different setting and lets you see the athletes in a different setting.

This is especially critical in the college setting because the athletes have just left high school where, for the most part, they have been surrounded by their family, friends and the community they know. There is a comfort level that comes with that. Finding ways to get your athletes out of the competitive atmosphere so they can get to know one another and their coaches better, and start to develop trust in one another off the field is very important because that trust will translate onto the field.

We have had teams use a ropes course, go white water rafting, work on a Habitat for Humanity project, and a number of other things. There really isn't a right and wrong way to do it, you just want to incorporate opportunities for your team to get together and get to know each other and the coaches in a different, non-competitive light just like you would schedule a drill into a practice. These occasions really help build trust, which is the foundation of all great teams.

LEAD, EDUCATE AND THEN GET OUT OF THEIR WAY

Great coaches are organized and able to communicate. Most importantly, they cherish and work hard at their role as a leader. You have to be able to bring players and coaches together. At the same time, as a head coach, you have to be great at delegating, educating people clearly on what you want done and then trusting that people will do their jobs, because you cannot do it all. You have to trust that you have hired the right people, given them the right direction as to where the ship is sailing and that this is the direction our team or department is going, and then support them in getting their job done.

LEARN FROM YOUR MISTAKES

You have to know that people are going to make mistakes; nobody is perfect. However, we have to learn from our mistakes and be able to "flush" them and get on to the next thing; utilizing what we have learned from those mistakes will make us better the next time the same or a similar situation arises. The best thing you can do with a mistake is own up to it, learn from it, and then let it go. We say that failure is positive feedback. If you can learn from your failures and use that information to make you and your team better, are they really failures?

David Bennett, former football coach at Coastal, had his team step into a bucket of water after practice one day and then asked them if anyone was able to walk on water? Nobody raised their hand. He told them that if you were perfect and were going to be perfect on every play that you would have been able to walk on water. He said that if you fell through the water and hit plastic, that you must be able to forgive, learn and forget. You must be able to move on to the next play because you are going to make mistakes; you are not going to be perfect.

GIVE YOURSELF THE BEST CHANCE FOR SUCCESS

You are not going to win every game. The goal is to give yourself and your team the best chances to win. If you can do that, you have done everything you can do. That is the ultimate success. That is something that John Wooden at UCLA used to talk about all the time: the process of success, the preparation, giving yourself the best chance to perform your best, and then trusting your preparation. He hardly ever talked about winning as a result; he spoke about it more as a daily goal, to give your best effort in everything that you did, to give yourself the best chance for success was the ultimate goal. To be prepared and then to execute to the best of your ability was the ultimate success, not what the scoreboard said at the end of the day.

ONE THING AT A TIME

It's funny how, regardless of the sport, it is usually one play in a game that will make the difference. If you look at our baseball team versus South Carolina in the NCAA Super Regional in 2010, you could say it was one hit in game one and one pitch in game two that made a difference. After the game you never know when that one pitch or one hit actually occurred, but the fans focus is always at the end of the game.

During the game there are multiple turning points and you never know when that pitch or that play is going to occur, so you have to be ready for every play and for every pitch. You have to be ready and truly play one play or one pitch at a time. You can't worry about the last one and can't stress over the future ones, it is all about the one in the moment – and that is where all of your focus needs to be.

PRACTICE MAKES PERMANENT

Most people think that practice makes perfect or that perfect practice makes perfect play. Unfortunately, I am still searching for someone who is perfect and for a coach that has had a perfect practice. I think we use the word perfect too much in athletics. We need to talk realistically and talk about giving our athletes and our team the best chance for success.

I have a fifteen-year-old son who plays baseball. We go to the field and I will hit him ground balls. He will make five throws great and then make a few errant throws. He will then say to me on the ride home "Dad, it doesn't matter. It's only practice". I try to tell him that making that throw in a game should be second nature to him because he has done it so many times in practice the right way that it is permanent when you get into a game situation. Practice makes permanent. You will play the way you practice. He needs to prepare so well that he isn't even thinking about it when the time comes to make that play in a game. He can trust himself and make the play because he has made it in practice before. The only way you can do that is if you practice at a high level of intensity and under game-like conditions.

One of the things I have him do is watch a game and time, on a stopwatch, the runner going to first base from the time the ball is hit to the time he steps on first base. If the average runner is 4.0 seconds then he knows if he is going to get anybody out he needs to field the ball and throw it to first base in under 4.0 seconds from when the ball is hit.

Once he sees this and understands the time association with making a play, we can then use the stopwatch in practice to try and get him to make plays in under 4.0 seconds. If he can do that in practice, then there is transfer to the game and there is no stepping up in a game, it's just doing what you do every practice. That is just one example of practice making permanent and developing trust in your skills.

APPLY SPORT SKILLS TO LIFE

One of the great things about athletics is that there are

so many things a coach can draw from between the lines to help the young people they lead in their life outside of athletics. How to manage your time, balance your schedule, be a part of a team, and work together with people with whom you may not have anything in common than except that you are on a team and are part of a shared vision for something bigger than yourself.

I think it is probably old-fashioned, but that's why athletics were invented in the first place; to teach student-athletes life lessons that will help them when their playing days are over. Coaches who can keep this in the forefront of their minds, while still preparing to put forth their best effort between the lines, are the coaches I have been around that are the most successful. That is because the life skills they teach through athletics, help their athletes to become better young men and women which helps them to perform better between the lines. You could say that winning, as an end result, is a by-product of teaching young people maturity, commitment to team goals, and, above all, how to live their lives the right way.

KEY POINTS FOR REVIEW:

- Coaches and athletes must commit to a common goal. Getting everyone on the same page is critical to a program's success. Establishing a goal setting process generates ownership of the goal by the whole program.

- Caring for athletes as people first and athletes second is necessary if they are going to follow your lead. Establish personal relationship that will allow you to get the most out of their potential.

- Utilize the strengths of other people in your program and in your community.

- As a leader, you must be able to educate people on what you want accomplished, delegate the responsibilities to them, and then trust that they will do it.

- Mistakes are not losses, they are learning opportunities. If you can learn from your mistakes you will speed up your learning curve and get the most out of your ability.

- As a coach, help your athletes to make the connection of how the sport skills they are learning can apply to life after sport. The majority of people who we coach will not go on and make a living in sport, but can hopefully make a life with the skills we have taught them through athletics.

> *Visit www.SoWhatNextPitch.com/EXTRAS*
> *For BONUS Mental Conditioning Material &*
> *FREE Peak Performance Training Tools*

Chapter 4 | TIPS FROM THE TRENCHES WITH PHILIP O'NEAL

Successful Director of Athletics

Shares Experience In Building Championship Programs

Philip O'Neal is the Director of Athletics for the Ft. Bend School District in Ft. Bend, Texas. He has served as a high school athletic director for over fifteen years and as a high school basketball coach for over twenty years. This chapter shares his experience in building championship programs.

STRENGTH AND CONDITIONING ARE ESSENTIAL

One of my favorite quotes is "There is no substitute for strength and no excuse for a lack of it". Strength is one of the only things that you can control in athletic performance and development. One of the best things you can do for your athletes is to get them on a great strength and conditioning program. Teaching the fundamentals of your sport is expected. But if you can also develop the physicality of your athletes you will really be setting yourself up for success.

Strength and conditioning has taken on one of the biggest evolutions in my career. The size, strength, and speed of the high school athletes today is far greater than it has ever been and I think that is directly related to the emphasis on strength and conditioning now at the high school level. Some schools have full-time strength and conditioning coaches but the majority of them do not. If you don't have a strength and conditioning coach, it is the head coaches' responsibility to get the training necessary to help develop their athletes.

There is also no substitute for mental toughness. A common mistake among coaches is the belief that mental toughness is a trait you are born with or that is in your DNA. However, mental toughness is a skill that you learn. Athletes acquire mental toughness through training and practice, just like the physical skills of their sport. Great coaches have a physical strength and conditioning program, but they also have an extensive mental conditioning program. Having a physical and mental conditioning program allows the athlete to fully develop to their potential.

PASSION IS CONTAGIOUS

The best coaches are passionate about teaching their sport. They are also able to share and portray that passion with their athletes and get them to develop a similar passion. I think that this is a missing ingredient for a lot of coaches. There are a lot of coaches who may be passionate and have great X and O knowledge, but they are unable to portray that passion and get people fired up about participating in their program. If you are not fired up with enthusiasm about teaching your sport, you will be fired with enthusiasm because you will not be very good.

MANAGEMENT IS A SKILL

The ability to manage all aspects of a program and especially to manage the ego and emotions of their players and staff is a trait of successful coaches. If you look at some of the great Major League Baseball managers, they are guys that can manage the clubhouse and manage the personalities.

It is often not the best team that wins, but the team that plays the best who does and part of playing the best is having a cohesive team and a chemistry that comes from having a leader that can get everyone pulling on the same end of the rope and get everyone to move in one direction together.

Great coaches also manage their time and excel at being both efficient and effective. Time management is more than just time management in their professional lives or in their job. It is also critical in managing the time with their team and family.

Sometimes your team needs a break. Great coaches have the ability to recognize that they are tired and that they need a break. Great coaches also recognize when their team needs to be pushed a little bit harder. A team that has too much early success where things are going a bit too good, often needs to get pushed and have the edge knocked off a bit. Sometimes losing early is a blessing because it keeps you hungry and motivates you to keep working so that you peak at the right time, at the end of the season.

Some coaches are successful everywhere they go because they understand those things. They understand the importance of attitude. If you are not managing your time well as a coach then you become fatigued and that fatigue comes out at practice and you may be a little on edge that day and that spills over to your team.

I think a lot of coaches fail to recognize the importance of having a balance and being able to manage their time personally and professionally so that they can be present at their job, with their team and most importantly, present with their families. Great coaches are also great actors.

Regardless of how their day is going they show up in front of their team with a positive attitude.

TUG ON THE SAME END OF THE ROPE

When you are dealing with athletes, especially at the high school level and below, you have athletes with many different motivations for playing. Some want to be with their friends, be recognized by their peers, be a part of a group, some want to be the best they can be and get to the next level, some play because their parents want them to, some play because that is what they have always done. Great coaches are able to take all those levels of commitment and get each individual to tug on the same end of the rope for a common cause.

INVEST TIME IN YOUR RELATIONSHIPS

To get those athletes to tug on the same end of the rope is a talent. One of the best things coaches can do to get their athletes to tug on the same end of the rope is to invest time in the relationship with the athlete off of the field.

Coaches must be very clear with their athletes that when they get upset with them at practice, it's not personal. They are upset with them as an athlete, them as a performer, not necessarily them as a person. The younger the athlete, the most important it is to talk with them about this.

When practice is over, practice is over. At that point, they are no longer the athlete, they are a person and as a coach you can't let what someone does as an athlete affect how you treat them as a person, that is personalizing performance and that will jeopardize your effectiveness as a coach.

Great coaches build into their practice plans, to hang out in the locker room or to talk with a specific athlete. Putting this in your practice plan accomplishes two things. One, it provides you with supervision of the locker room and two, it gives your athletes an opportunity to see you as coaches outside of a competitive environment and to see you as people, not just this guy that comes to work, coaches us and then goes home.

The best way to get to know your own children is to spend quality time with them. This also helps you to figure out what makes them tick, what their motivations are, and what their interest and commitment to the program really is.

ROLE PLAYERS ARE IMPORTANT

When we used to watch film I would often ask a player after watching himself execute something well how he was able to do that and their response was usually "Because I work on it in practice." I would then use that as an opportunity to point out that the reason they were able to do that in a game was because there was someone at practice pushing them every day to get better.

I would then ask them to make a point and go thank the backup players who push them in practice and help make them better. This experience humbles the starter a bit and validates the backup player, which is huge for motivating them to continue working.

COACHING FOR SIGNIFICANCE OR SUCCESS

There are those coaches that want to be successful and those that want to be significant. Those that want to be successful want to be known as a "Coach of the Year" or because they won a state championship and those that want to be significant want to be remembered as being important in the lives of the people who they serve. The funny thing is, the coaches that try to be significant will experience more end result success than those who try to be successful because end result winning is a by-product of doing things the right way and a by-product of teaching and developing the athletes you serve.

The best coaches are the ones that create a positive experience for their athletes and will then step back and watch the kids get all the credit for their hard work and success. The coaches who coach for significance are focusing on the process and on working each and every day on empowering their athletes to do what is right. They step back and say how proud they are of their athletes for what they have accomplished. Great coaches give the wins to the athletes and take the losses as their own.

BAYLOR BASKETBALL JOYRIDE

In 2005 when the Baylor University Bears won the National Championship in women's basketball, their coach Kim Mulkey constantly talked about the journey being more important than the destination and the wonderful ride that her players had been taking her on. It wasn't about her; it was about the people she served. She talked about how fortunate she was to be a part of those players and the experience.

SAY WHAT YOU MEAN, MEAN WHAT YOU SAY

Great coaches say what they mean and mean what they say. Accountability is key on championship teams. If you, as a coach, have a rule or a policy, you need to enforce it or you lose all of your credibility. Unfortunately, discipline often has a negative connotation to it with the high school athlete and discipline is one of the key characteristics of all great programs. Discipline is following through with what you said you were going to do.

Tom Landry, the Hall of Fame coach of the Dallas Cowboys, was known for always being in control of himself and never losing his cool. His players never wanted to disappoint or let him down and they never wanted to break any rules because if they did, they knew that Landry was going to follow through with the consequences.

That is what accountability is all about. It is drawing a line in the sand and saying, here is the standard and here are the consequences. I am not going to scream and yell at you, it is not going to be a debate, if you break our standard of excellence, I am going to move on and you will serve the consequences. There will not be a lot of discussion.

As with any mistake there are three things that need to happen.

1) Admit you were wrong.

2) Take responsibility for your actions, learn from your mistake, and serve the consequence.

3) Forgive yourself and move on.

Landry's players feared his wrath, but his wrath was simply follow through and accountability to the standards of excellence he set for his team. Follow through is essential for your credibility. There is no gray area. There are standards of excellence and people need to meet that standard or they need to be held accountable, or you as the coach lose all credibility. That is why many coaches will have very few rules so that they can handle each situation on a case-by-case basis.

MENTAL TOUGHNESS

A significant competitive advantage goes to the coaches who can focus in the moment and let go of the distractions. Distractions happen all the time. You are coaching on the sidelines, there is a parent bad-mouthing you from the stands, the game is starting to get away from you on the scoreboard because of an officials bad call. With adversity you can either get frustrated and discouraged or get fascinated and encouraged.

You and your team are either going to perform better or worse under the pressure. There will always be pressure. Get used to it. The best coaches are the ones that can focus on the moment and let go of the distractions. They let go of the distractions by focusing on what they can control and by focusing on the moment.

CONTROL WHAT YOU CAN CONTROL

Coaches have a choice. They can focus on what they can control or focus on what they can't. Unfortunately too many coaches get stuck focusing on the things that they can't control versus getting into the things they can. This is what mental toughness is all about.

This is hard to do when you are young and inexperienced, but many older coaches fail to recognize that they are focusing on things that they can't control. Learning to focus on what you can control is a skill that can be developed, but is difficult to master. Those that can are well served by being able to focus on what they can control and by being able to let go of things they can't.

NO EXCUSES

Great coaches also refuse to make excuses. They take the cards they are dealt and still take the perspective that they can win the game. They don't complain about the kids who are ineligible or are hurt, they just play the hand they are dealt and make the most of it. They realize that you can make excuses or make it happen, but you can't do both.

One of the most successful high school football coaches in Texas talks about playing every play to the best of our ability and letting the scoreboard take care of itself. He says that if they execute every play to the best of their ability, they should deserve to win. He doesn't want his players and staff focusing on the scoreboard, he wants them to focus on the moment and on playing this play, another example of mental toughness.

He also talks about how the best team never wins, but it is the team that plays the best who always does. I think he has one of the most talented teams physically, but he is on another level mentally with getting them to play one play at a time. When you have talent and mental toughness, you are going to be very successful. Unfortunately, we can't always control the talent, but we can teach the mental toughness.

BE A COACH OF COACHES

Great coaches are also constantly coaching their coaches. You have to share your experiences with the coaches on your staff and with youth coaches in your sport. You want to share those experiences with them so that they can learn from you and then do the things that you want them to do better. The better you can educate your assistants the better your athletes will be. You will get more mileage out of your assistants and they will enjoy their journey more if you take the time to coach them and go over every detail of how you want them to do things. A common mistake is for the head coach to try and do everything themselves either for egotistical reasons or because they do not know how to delegate. If you can't delegate, you will never reach the levels of success the best of the best do. You can't do everything yourself as a head coach.

KNOW WHO YOU ARE

There are no cookie cutter approaches to being a great coach. You have got to know who you are as a person and who you are as a coach. Some coaches are hard on kids and kids love them for it. Some coaches will be hard on kids and the kids hate their guts for it. This is often because they are not being who they truly are and are inconsistent with their coaching methods and in how they treat the people they serve.

You have to be who you are and who you are can be good enough as long as you follow through on the accountability piece and can portray your passion. You can be who you are and still have a lot of success. One of the traps that young coaches fall into is that they try to be who coached them instead of being themselves. It often takes time to figure out who you are as a coach. This is a journey that never ends.

Knowing who you are leads to consistency. Athletes have a great read for people who are trying to be someone they aren't. Athletes can see right through you when you are not consistent. They will chew you up and spit you out.

HERB BROOKS BEWARE

Sometimes you can use the tactic of getting people to spite you, to get them to tug on the same end of the rope. That is a tactic that Herb Brooks used with the 1980 USA Olympic Hockey Team. I don't recommend that as a tactic because it can really backfire on you, but I have seen it done.

KNOW YOUR PHILOSOPHY ON PLAYING TIME

When all things were equal with two players I used to play the one who was the oldest. I learned that when all things were equal, you need to play the athlete who works the hardest. When you have that type of philosophy, you will get kids who want to play so they work harder than they might if they knew you were going to play the older athlete and subsequently they become better at their sport.

The older athletes see the younger guys in the weight room or taking extra reps and they think, I have to stay longer because we are close in ability and if I don't, that younger guy is going to get my playing time. When you have this healthy competition amongst your team, good work habits will follow.

Rewarded behaviors are repeated behaviors and if you reward the behavior that you want as a coach (hard work) with what the athlete wants (playing time), you will get more of the behavior that you want.

CREATE COMPETITION IN PRACTICE

The most successful coaches have a lot of competition structured into their practices. There is a winner and loser for almost everything they do. Competing from the way they clean up the field after practice, under time and trying to break their record, to having a competition between players in drills; competitiveness is something that needs to be taught and worked on every day.

A key concept to remember is that measurement equals motivation. If you want athletes to be motivated, you have to measure what they do in practice and chart their progress. When you have athletes compete and it's measured and posted, it sharpens their focus.

You can create competition by putting drills under time or by setting statistical goals for people to strive for. If you are not competing and setting a goal for each drill, athletes will just go through the motions. There is nothing to measure their progress against.

Athletes need to recognize and reward the people who help them to do what they do in team sports. The selfless, sacrificial behavior of a lineman in football who will take on a player so that a linebacker can make a tackle in the gap, or the basketball player who sets the pick to free up their teammate to get an open shot, those behaviors often go unnoticed, but those are the critical behaviors that must be rewarded.

PEOPLE DON'T CARE WHAT YOU KNOW UNTIL THEY KNOW YOU CARE

Coaches that truly care about the people who they serve will also get more out of them. One of the oldest clichés is, "people don't care what you know until they know that you care". That is very true in the coaching profession.

There has to be respect as well. It is better to be respected than liked, but I think the two go hand in hand. If you will be yourself when you are coaching and will set standards of excellence for people to live up to, hold them accountable and teach mental toughness, you will get people holding onto the same end of the rope and get the most out of the people who you serve.

KEY POINTS FOR REVIEW:

If coaches are going to be successful they should know:

- **Strength and conditioning are essential parts of any successful program, and if they don't have a strength coach, they need to create a program that they can implement.**

- **Energy and passion is contagious, make sure yours is positive.**

- **Management is a skill – always be working to improve your time, personal, and interpersonal management skills.**

- **The importance of working to get everyone in your organization tugging on the same end of the rope.**

- **The value of investing time into relationships with your players.**

- **That backup players are important part of your program, make sure they feel validated in their role.**

- **The importance of saying what you mean and meaning what you say. Your words are powerful.**

- **Mental toughness is a skill that can be taught.**

- **The importance of controlling what you can control.**

- **That you should accept no excuses from yourself or the people you teach.**

- That if you are a high school varsity coach and want to be successful year after year, you need to be coaching the coaches in your community who are coaching at the k-12 levels. The sooner they all can learn your system and terminology the more quickly athletes will learn and progress..

- Who you are and what you believe in.

- Your philosophy on playing time.

- How to create competition in practice.

- People don't care what you know until they know that you care.

PART 2

How They Do It:
Masters of The Mental Game Share Mental Conditioning Strategies & Tips

Chapter 5 | MEETING A GRANDMASTER
OF MENTAL CONDITIONING

A Day with Harvey Dorfman

During the summer of 1998 I was pitching for the Eastern Tides (Connecticut) of the New England Collegiate Baseball League. I was a struggling pitcher from the University of Vermont, trying to find my pitching abilities that had seemed to vanish since I had graduated from high school. My roommate was Mike Levy, a catcher from Dartmouth College. The book he left on the table that changed my life forever was The Mental Game of Baseball by H.A. Dorfman.

I remember picking up The Mental Game of Baseball and not being able to put it down. That was a first. The Mental Game of Baseball was the first book I remember reading from cover to cover. It grabbed me and held my attention like no other book had up to that point in my life.

I was looking for something or someone who would help me turn my career around. Unfortunately for me, I got injured and my career was over shortly thereafter. Maybe I would have had a more successful outcome if I had been turned on to the mental game at an earlier age.

I had a great work ethic, was a good teammate, and had a great passion to be successful. That was the biggest problem. I wanted it TOO much. I wanted to be so good that I couldn't get out of my own way.

Reading The Mental Game of Baseball inspired me to

explore the mental aspects of the game. I read Dorfman's six other books, *The Mental ABC's of Pitching*, *The Mental Keys to Hitting*, *Coaching The Mental Game*, and his anecdotal memories *Persuasion of My Days, Each Needle, Each Branch* and *Copying It Down*. These books captivated me and motivated me to pursue a degree in Sport Psychology with the author of another tremendous mental game book called *Heads-Up Baseball*, by Dr. Ken Ravizza.

Ken Ravizza is one of the most influential people in my life and genuine grandmaster of the mental game. He has been a true friend and mentor, but I will never forget the first taste of the mental game I received from Harvey Dorfman and *The Mental Game of Baseball*.

Ten years after first reading The Mental Game of Baseball, through a mutual friend, I was able to spend a day with Dorfman. Below are the highlights and inexpensive experience I gained from meeting one of my greatest heroes, the man who was responsible for providing me the first step towards my life's mission of being a successful teacher of the mental game.

AWARENESS – STRATEGY – ACTION

One of the foundations of the mental game that Dorfman talked about was the development of the athlete's self-awareness. This self-awareness involves the athlete being conscious of his/her self-talk and game-time thoughts and extends to an awareness of the situations that put the athlete into a poor mental state.

He said, "Once athletes have an awareness of what they are thinking and feeling, they can do something to change it. *What you are aware of, you can control. What you are unaware of will control you.* Getting athletes and coaches to become aware of what they do to perform at their best is equally important as to get them to know what they are doing when they perform at less than their best."

Once you have an awareness of what is hurting your performance, the next step is to develop a strategy to get you back into your peak performing state.

"Once athletes are aware, they can develop strategies to shift their thinking to something that is going to be task-relevant and help their performance," Dorfman said. "Once athletes are aware, the goal is to educate them on a strategy they can use to perform better. There is no uniform strategy that will work for all athletes in every situation. *There is no cookbook approach to sport psychology.* It is about knowing the athletes and finding a strategy that works for them."

Once the athlete has self-awareness and a strategy to use, the final piece of the performance puzzle is to IMPLEMENT the strategy. I often use the example: K-A=0. Knowledge minus action equals no change. ACTION must take place for there to be any performance improvement. Implementation of the strategy must happen.

"When an athlete has awareness and a strategy, he must USE the strategy that he has." Dorfman said. "As a Mental Game coach, once the athlete has developed self-awareness and we have worked to develop a strategy, it becomes the athlete's responsibility to implement it. Nobody can do that for them. It's the responsibility of the man in the arena to use what he knows."

WHO DO YOU LISTEN TO?

When an athlete reaches the pinnacle of his career, the highest levels of his professional sport, people will come out of the woodwork to try and become a part of his success. One thing that successful athletes need to learn is who they should listen to and who they should let go in one ear and out the other.

"Many times coaches will try to change a pitcher's or a player's mechanics to do something the way the coach wants him to because then the coach can satisfy his ego by taking some of the credit for the success of the athlete," Dorfman said. "If a player is good enough to make it to the upper echelon of sport, he has found a way that works for him. It may not look great, and it may not be the most 'economical' way, scientifically, but if it works for the athlete and it is the athlete's natural mechanic, why change it?"

"Athletes and coaches need to use a filter when listening to others who have their own best interest in mind, not the best interest of the athlete."

CONSTANT REMINDERS

One of the things I hear all the time in my work with athletes is "Cain, you always tell us the same things." As a young Mental Game coach, I then try to find new ways to teach the same material, or find other areas of the Mental Game to explore, but the reason I'm having the conversation with the athlete in the first place is because he isn't doing what he knows.

"The two words I hear the most are 'I Know.' I hear that all the time," Dorfman said. "The athlete has to understand that *it is not what they know that matters, it is what they do that counts.* If they know what to do, but don't do what they know, they are no better off than the person who has no clue about what to do."

It's the constant repetitions of the basic Mental Game fundamentals that lead to success over the course of the player's career. I think Rod Delmonico, former head coach at the University of Tennessee, and Dave Serrano, the current head coach at Tennessee, said it best when they said: "Baseball is a marathon, not a sprint."

Many athletes know what to do, but over the course of running their marathon and playing their season, they forget some of the fundamental Mental Game skills, such as routines and deep breathing. Often all they need is a quick "brain tune-up" or reminder of what they already know but are not doing.

COMPETE IN THE MOMENT, LIVE IN THE BIG PICTURE

One of the concepts that Dorfman stressed to me is that athletes play at their best when they play in the present moment. When you live in the moment and play one pitch at a time, you give yourself the best chance for success. With the pressures of moving up through the minor leagues, or through the college- recruiting process, players can often get pulled mentally in all different directions.

"One of the common faults I see with baseball players is that they get caught thinking about things that are outside their realm of control," Dorfman said. *"When players are doing great they are playing in the moment, but living in the big picture.* They understand the politics of professional baseball and realize that so many factors are outside of their control."

"When athletes struggle, they will play in the big picture of things and see statistical situations such as 'If I go 2-for-3 today I will be hitting over .300.' And they live in the moment, which can cause stress. For example, they overanalyze when one of their teammates gets called up and they wonder why they were not the one to get the promotion. Athletes perform at their best when they play in the moment, pitch by pitch, and live in the big picture, focusing on the long-term goals of their career, and when they don't get caught up in the day-to-day politics and things outside of their control."

RELAXED MUSCLES & AGGRESSIVE MENTALITY

When baseball players struggle it can often be linked to two factors: the player is competing with tension in his muscles or playing with a passive mentality. The best players in the game compete with relaxed muscles and an aggressive mentality.

"When players struggle they will often be looking for the perfect pitch or try to make the perfect pitch and can compete with a passive mentality," Dorfman said. "That is a recipe for disaster. Athletes want to play with a relaxed intensity. They want aggression in their mind but relaxation in their bodies. The athletes that look like they're playing with an ease about them have figured this out."

BE PAINFULLY HONEST

One concept that truly described Dorfman's coaching style was his encouragement to be painfully honest. There is not enough time to beat around the bush and tip-toe around in an effort to avoid pissing people off. If you want to be an effective coach, you must get to the core quickly and be willing to call people on their bullshit.

"There just is not enough time to dance around the issues. You need to call a spade a spade and get right to the point," Dorfman said. "Athletes want and need that. They will respect you as a coach for saving them the time and cutting through the crap. Get to the core of the issue. Get to the point because that is the only time that progress can be made."

ROUTINES EASE PLAYER ANTICIPATION

When athletes have to wait around for a competition to start, they can often psych themselves out by over analyzing due to the anticipation of the competition. Often you will see this manifest in a pitcher struggling in the first inning, only to turn it around and pitch well for the rest of the game. The problem is that by this time it may already be too late.

"The anticipation for the athlete can often be more stressful and tiresome than the actual game," claims Dorfman. "Athletes need to develop strategies and skills that they can use to take their mind off the game and off of things they can't control."

"Once you get into the flow of the game, it's easy. Having a routine in place that you go through to help you separate and segment from being the athlete to being the person outside of the athlete will help to minimize stress, minimize the pressure and anticipation, and allow you to play at your best when it's needed most."

TRIBUTE TO A LEGEND

Meeting Dorfman was one of the most valuable experiences of my career. His willingness to share his inexpensive experience was greatly appreciated and I have been able to successfully implement many of his strategies for teaching mental toughness. His teaching model of awareness, strategy and action has been a game changer for me and the athletes I work with in the field of Mental Conditioning. Dorfman passed away on February 28, 2011. He touched the lives of many people, myself included, and paved the way for mental conditioning.

I want to thank my good friend Tim "Cowboy" Brown for arranging my opportunity to meet Dorfman and his wonderful wife Anita at their North Carolina home. It was truly a life changing experience. I encourage the reader to seek out and pursue meeting your mentors and people who are the grandmasters in your field. I also encourage the reader to explore Dorfman's seven books, which are all cornerstones of my library.

- The Mental ABC's of Pitching: A Handbook for Performance Enhancement by H. A. Dorfman

- The Mental Keys to Hitting: A Handbook of Strategies for Performance Enhancement by Dorfman

- The Mental Game of Baseball: A Guide to Peak Performance by Dorfman and Karl Kuehl

- Persuasion of My Days: An Anecdotal Memoir: The Early Years by Dorfman

- Coaching the Mental Game: Leadership Philosophies and Strategies for Peak Performance in Sports and Everyday Life by Dorfman.

- Copying It Down: An Anecdotal Memoir: Sport as Art by Dorfman

- Each Branch, Each Needle: An Anecdotal Memoir: The Final Stories by Dorfman

KEY POINTS FOR REVIEW:

- Develop an awareness of what you do when you perform at your best and at your worst, and develop a strategy to get into to your peak-performing state.

- Play in the moment, pitch by pitch, but live in the big picture, focusing on long-term goals and not getting caught up in day-to-day things that are beyond your control.

- Compete with relaxed muscles and an aggressive mentality.

- Develop strategies for dealing with the time spent waiting for a competition to start because the anticipation is often worse than the participation.

Visit www.SoWhatNextPitch.com/EXTRAS
For BONUS Mental Conditioning Material &
FREE Peak Performance Training Tools

Chapter 6 | A TRUE HERO IN BASEBALL AND THE GAME OF LIFE

Eric Degre Coaches Character from the Dugout and the Fire House

D edication, commitment, teamwork, strong work ethic, sacrifice, putting others ahead of yourself, facing fears head-on; these are all desired traits that we look for in players and coaches in the game of baseball.

Eric Degre, a high school baseball educator in Vermont has also served as the Chief of the Newport City, Vermont Fire Department. He's a man dedicated to teaching life lessons to the youth in his community, and lives by setting an example both on and off the field. *Athletes need a model to see more than they need a motto to say* and Coach Degre has served as that model for his players.

"If I were to teach these young men only how to throw and hit, I would be doing them and the game of baseball a disservice," Degre said. "My job first and foremost is to teach them how to be better young men and how to be positive, contributing members of society. Most of the players we coach will never make a dime playing this game, but if I can get them to love the game, learn to make a commitment to their teammates, and give everything they have every day in trying to get better, we will be successful regardless of what the scoreboard says at the end of the day."

WINNING IS A BY-PRODUCT

Degre understands what is so often lost in coaching these days: that winning is a by-product of doing things well.

"If these boys will truly make the commitment to each other and to the game, the success on the field will take care of itself. We cannot control what the scoreboard says at the end of the day, all we can control is how we play the game. If we play the game as well as we're capable of, and play it pitch-by-pitch, we are giving ourselves the best chance for success. I try to get them to realize that in baseball, as in life, you can do everything right, and still not get your desired outcome. This is a game of failure, you have to look at more than the results. You have to be able to look at the man in the mirror and know that you didn't let him down. You have to know that you did everything you were capable of doing. That is success."

LEADING BY EXAMPLE

Leading by example is something that all effective leaders will do. Many coaches ask their players to treat umpires and the game with respect, but often fail to lead by example and practice what they preach. As the Chief of the Newport City, Vermont Fire Department, Degre often makes connections between life in the firehouse and life between the lines, hoping that his players will have a better understanding that what they learn on the field will help them later in life.

"As a fireman, you have to be willing to run into a burning building when everyone else is running out. That takes a lot of training, preparation, and, most importantly, a large amount of trust in the other men, that if you go in together, you are all coming out together," Degre said. "That trust is not just given. You cannot have confidence in your team if you have not shed a lot of blood, sweat, and tears with them through the preparation process. It is the same in baseball. How can you completely trust one of your teammates if you or they have taken shortcuts or done less than your best in the weight room or during practice?"

"We use the term 'hold the hose' as a fire department. 'Hold the hose' means that when you go into a fire, everyone is in it together. If you let go of the hose, you are letting go of one of your brothers and that can't happen. I really believe that when you hear championship teams say that they had great chemistry, they really mean that they had unconditional trust in each other."

FIREFIGHTING AND BASEBALL GO HAND IN HAND

"Firefighting is a lot like baseball. There are so many things that you can't control. You have to learn to stay in control of yourself at all times and *be comfortable being uncomfortable.* At a fire, or an accident, it might be a friend, family member, or a student whom I've had in class. I have to be able to stay in control of myself and not get caught up in the emotion of the moment, or I might do something that could injure myself or one of my teammates. In baseball, you have to stay in control of yourself at all times or you might end up giving away an at-bat, or making a pitch that you're not fully committed to. In either case of firefighting or baseball, the end result can be less than desired. The benefit of baseball is that you usually get to play again the next day."

PLAYERS APPRECIATE EFFORTS

The players who play for Degre know that he is as genuine and caring as any coach in the game today. Although they may not know it while they are playing for him, because he demands so much of them, by the time they are ready to graduate, most have figured out that what they have learned between the lines will benefit them later in life.

"Coach Degre is the best coach I have ever played for," former player Anthony Bonvechio said. "His passion for the game is contagious, he challenges you to get better every day, and he is always out in front showing us how to do it. We may be dog tired, but if Coach is still out there doing it, we have to continue to push ourselves. What he teaches us not only helps us on the baseball field, but in the classroom and outside of school as well."

"Coach Degre taught me how to be a better baseball player and a better person," said former shortstop Sean Pare. "His dedication to the game and to us is something that I will never forget. He taught me more about life than I thought I ever would learn playing high-school sports."

FOCUS IS ON MORE THAN JUST BASEBALL

"You have to admire and respect a man who gives so much back to the community and does so with such enthusiasm and energy," North Country Union High School Principal Bill Rivard said. "Eric has done a great job at rejuvenating baseball at our school and in the community. He cares about the kids more than just as baseball players; he sincerely cares about them as people. He is constantly checking in with them about their grades and sees to it that they give their best effort on and off the field. Eric does a great job in teaching life lessons through sport, which is something that is extremely important to me as an administrator."

TEACHING LIFE LESSONS THROUGH SPORT

One way that Degre would try to teach life lessons through sport was to hold weekly meetings on the Mental Game of Baseball. This became a time to stress the importance of drawing life lessons from the game and a time to focus on the character development of his players, an idea he developed from attending the American Baseball Coaches Association National Convention.

"I have gone to the ABCA National Convention for years and one of the best things I took away from the convention and the opportunity to collaborate with lots of great coaches was the importance of coaching for character," Degre said. "I realized that I was trying to teach life lessons, but might be more successful if I took a more direct approach and really laid it out there for the players that this is what I expect you are learning from playing in this program, and these are the standards of excellence that you are expected to live up to."

"We would meet on Wednesdays for an hour or so. I would always buy them pizza just to make sure they would stay motivated to be there, and we would talk about the parallels between the game and life. We would talk about how most of the time we can't control the outcome, but always have a lot of control over the process."

"We would talk about the importance of having a good handshake and looking people in the eye when you talk with them, and how they are viewed differently than other people in the school and community because they are athletes and have a duty to be responsible and polite in and out of school."

"We ordered polo shirts that say North Country Baseball on them, and the players wear them to school every game day. I want them to take pride in being a member of the baseball program and in carrying themselves as a part of the team."

"We also spent time developing and discussing our program mission. I let them have a say in the development of the mission because if they are able to be a part of the development, it becomes their mission and they hold each other accountable. The discipline issues take a turn for the better and the guys really get behind what it is they are expected to strive for. It has been a lot of fun to see their development as young men."

"QUOTE OF THE DAY" – A PROGRAM FOR SUCCESS

One of the ways in which Degre gets his players to think about the life lessons learned through baseball is to hang a quote of the day on the bulletin board in the locker room every morning before school. *He also hangs the practice plan for the day so players can look at the board during the school day when they have a free moment and start mentally preparing for the day's practice.*

"I would hang a quote each day. I would hang them at 6:30 in the morning on my way into work. The quotes would sometimes be motivational from great baseball players like Greg Maddux, Roger Clemens, or Pete Rose, or they might be on the comic side from Yogi Berra or someone totally non-related to baseball," Degre said "I would then start practice each day by asking the players what the quote of the day was and how it applied to them on a personal level and what we were trying to do as a baseball team."

"They could almost always make a connection to the team and usually it was in a way that hadn't even occurred to me. The quote of the day exposed them to some great minds and some great books. Great leaders like John Wooden, Helen Keller, Henry Ford, people that our players may not have really known a lot about. We are always trying to introduce them to some of the amazing leaders, coaches, and people out there who they can look to as motivators and people who they should strive to be like, people who, from my perspective, have done a great job of 'holding the hose.'"

KEY POINTS FOR REVIEW:

- A coach's job, first and foremost, is to teach his players how to become positive, contributing members of society.

- In baseball, as in life, you can do everything right and still not achieve your desired result; success is doing everything you are capable of doing.

- Players need a model to see more than a motto to say.

- Hang a practice plan and a quote of the day on a bulletin board, then start practice by asking about the quote and how it applies to what you're trying to accomplish.

Chapter 7 | BASEBALL'S MOST MENTALLY TOUGH FAN

Hall of Fame Wrestling Coach Dan Gable
Shares Insight On Coaching Mental Toughness
From the Mat to the Dugout

I had the opportunity to see Hall-of-Fame wrestling coach Dan Gable's presentation "Creating Mental Toughness on the Mat" and tried to adapt some of his mental-toughness training techniques for the baseball diamond.

Gable's success is legendary. He was an Olympic Gold Medalist, won an amazing fifteen National Championships as head wrestling coach at the University of Iowa, and was the three-time winner of the NCAA National Coach of The Year award.

In this chapter I'll relate the mental-toughness tips Gable shared and include some of the current techniques I'm using with top mixed martial artists in the Ultimate Fighting Championship and top collegiate athletes across the country.

COACHES SET TONE FOR COMPETITION

My notes from Gable's presentation were filled with great quotes and impressive conditioning drills. One of the things he said that stuck out most was *"Great coaches get their kids nervous before practice because they know they're going to be put into competitive situations."*

As I look around collegiate and high-school baseball, the most successful programs I've had the opportunity to work with are also the most competitive programs on a daily basis, both at practice and in the weight room. The reason they're so competitive is that the head coach makes it that way. They talk about, and, more importantly, evaluate practice competition on a daily basis.

EXCELLENCE IS A DAILY ENDEAVOR

Gable also said, "You cannot pursue excellence in one area of life and fail to pursue excellence in another. You can fool yourself by thinking you can turn it on and off, but excellence and being a champion is a lifestyle, not an event. Being a champion is a way of life, not something you do from 2 to 5 p.m. when you step on the mat for practice."

As a peak performance coach I see athletes who all too often feel they can turn it on and off. They feel they can "flip the switch" when they step between the lines, but can turn it off in the classroom or at the nutritional training table. These athletes are fooling themselves. Excellence is founded in the routines of our daily lives.

According to Gable, "True champions compete with themselves to see how good they can be at everything they do. From working harder than anyone else, to being more nutritionally sound than anyone else, to being able to work harder at recovery and being willing to do the things like massage, stretching, and sauna that no one else wants to do."

COMPETE WITH SELF VS. OTHERS

Gable often spoke about competing with others but kept coming back to *the ultimate competition, which was with yourself, to see just how good you can be.*

I speak a lot more about competing with yourself than with others. As the great John Wooden said, "Success is not how good you are compared to other people, success is how good you are compared to how good you could be."

Mixed martial arts (MMA), wrestling, and baseball are all very different sports; but, despite the differences in rules, they share similar mental-game principals. One common thread is that you need to be mentally tough to succeed. The biggest difference I see is that in MMA and wrestling, you compete one-on-one. There is no teammate to pick you up if you make a bad pitch or fail to execute a sacrifice bunt. The action is fierce and non-stop for the entire match, and often it's the athlete with the superior will who defeats the athlete with the better skill.

In baseball, it's a different story. Your opponents are yourself, the ball, and the game. University of Texas coach Augie Garrido said it best in a College Sports Television (CSTV) special called Training Camp: "Your two biggest opponents in baseball are frustration and boredom. Right when you start to check out and lose your focus, the ball will be hit to you." Mental toughness in baseball is the ability to focus for 2-3 hours in 3-6 second segments. The combat athlete, on the other hand, has to focus continually for 1-25 minutes, depending on the length of the match.

The similarities of MMA and baseball are that you must be able to withstand, pressure, adversity and frustration. Not every move in the cage or pitch on the diamond is going to be successful. Often in either sport, it's the athlete that can stay focused in the moment and on the execution of fundamentals that will come out on top. By staying focused in the moment and challenging yourself to perform at your best, you give yourself the best chance for success.

INTENSE PRACTICE PREPARES FOR GAME TIME

Many coaches believe that mental training is making their athletes adhere to a strict, difficult, and physically demanding conditioning program. This is a big part of teaching mental toughness, but not the only part. One of the major problems I find with the perception that mental toughness can only obtained by demanding physical work is that athletes commonly fail to push their limits throughout practice. It is an unfortunate and all too common practice for players to save energy for the more difficult drills. This illustrates a failure to go all-out in every drill and for every pitch as we expect them to during games.

Gable strives to make his athletes crawl out the door, not walk out the door, when practice is over. On a daily basis, he wants his athletes to go through workouts that are more physically and mentally challenging in practice than they will ever face when they step on the mat for a match – a technique very similar to the one reportedly used by Coach Wooden at UCLA.

"I want our athletes to feel like they deserve to win because they're the hardest working group in the nation," Gable said. "It isn't enough to want to win. Wanting to win gets you nowhere. Deserving to win by pushing your physical and mental limits on a daily basis is what makes champions."

"Coaching mental toughness is an everyday thing. It's a philosophy. It's apparent in the things you do every day. From the way you dress, to the way you pick up after yourself when you finish eating, to the amount of effort you give in practice. You cannot pursue excellence in one area of life and fail to pursue excellence in every other aspect.

Excellence is an all-the- time commitment, not a part-time endeavor."

Having worked with *Ultimate Fighting Championship* welterweight champion Georges St. Pierre, Gable's philosophy echoes the necessity of physically and mentally demanding workouts. "The more you sweat in training, the less you bleed in the fight," St. Pierre often says.

MENTAL TOUGHNESS – THE MASTER KEY

Gable also said, "Mental toughness is the key of all keys, yet by itself it is not enough. You must also maximize your techniques, tactics, strength, conditioning, flexibility, nutrition, and recovery. Mental toughness is the foundation for all those things, but you must train them all as if they were the one thing that would win you a national championship."

"When you have ten sprints to do, the first sprint is the most important and the one where you must give all you have. Then the number 2 sprint becomes the most important and the hardest one. Then the number 3 sprint. It's about challenging yourself one sprint at a time and leaving it all on the mat. Through this conditioning we work to get our athletes to the point that when it gets down to the last 40 seconds of a match, they're not working to protect their lead, but working to increase it. We're always working to increase our lead and put pressure on our opponents. I see a lot of athletes who compete not to lose versus competing to win. That is a big mental mistake."

MENTAL CONDITIONING RESOURCES AVAILABLE

During his presentation Gable often read from one of his favorite books, *The Heart of a Champion* by Bob Richards.

Richards was an Olympic pole-vaulting champion and was the first athlete to grace the cover of a Wheaties cereal box.

Gable quoted from Richards book, "Wishful thinking will destroy many peoples' aspirations. You must have the will and the drive deep down in your gut to work hard and makes these wishes a reality."

Many of the collegiate, high-school, and professional players and teams I work with use my PRIDE – Personal Responsibility In Daily Excellence – program as their mental conditioning curriculum and as a way to help build their mental-toughness. The program provides a year-round system of mental-toughness training drills and worksheets for players, coaches, and teams to fill out and then discuss.

Chris Lavoie, a successful high school athletic director and baseball coach was one of the first coaches to implement the PRIDE program with his team.

Like many of the coaches I work with, Lavoie wanted to address that his team often competed better against a weaker opponent, but then struggled at playing their best when it was needed most, against a tougher opponent or one of equal ability.

"The PRIDE program helped our team eliminate the peaks and valleys that seem to be inevitable in baseball, and helped us play towards the top of our potential," Lavoie said. "We also improved at being able to win with humility and lose with dignity, which is a goal I try to get all of our kids to strive towards."

"The PRIDE program gave me some concrete ways to send the message to our team that in baseball you compete against the game and the ball, not the team in the other dugout. The goal is to play our game, one pitch at a time, in the present moment, with a positive mentality, and The PRIDE Program helped us accomplish that."

ACCOUNTABILITY IS ESSENTIAL

Gable said that one common trait in all the champions he has coached was the ability to push themselves when nobody was watching. They knew what to do when there was no coach around to tell them what to do. Knowing what to do if nobody shows up at practice, or if you're working out on your own, will allow you to get the most out of every day.

Gable demonstrated with two of his wrestlers just how difficult and demanding his warm-up was. "My warm-up is like most people's work out," he said. "I want our guys to be dripping with sweat before we start to practice because when I ask them to go from a heart rate of 80 beats per minute to 180 beats per minute, they better be ready or they will crash."

I see many high-intensity warm-up procedures now being used by top pitching coaches across the country. Many of these coaches demand that their pitchers take the time necessary to be more than warm and ready before they pick up a ball and start to pitch. Unfortunately, I still see pitchers running poles and static stretching as a means of warm-up instead of doing bands and other dynamic warm-up exercises to get their bodies and minds ready to compete. Coaches need to regularly attend clinics and learn what the research says is the best practice for their athletes.

GREATNESS STARTS IN THE MIND

Gable spoke of the importance of finding ways to make his practice sessions more like competition, so when it became time to compete, they would be better able to trust their training and compete at their best. The daily competition at practice drives his athletes to turn competition into a lifestyle, not an event.

"It may sound strange but many champions are champions because of setbacks," Gable said. "Sometimes in life it takes difficulties to bring out the fighting spirit in people. We try to put our team in those difficult situations every day. We try to get them to push through that breaking point. Life does not determine a champion, a champion determines life. You can never accept mediocrity in anything you do if you want to go far. If you think you can go higher, go higher."

"Why do people try to accomplish the impossible? Champions are driven by an instinctive impulse to reach the top. That is a place where all the great ones want to be and they compete every day with the type of mentality it takes to deserve to get there."

"To accomplish what has never been accomplished before, whether it be winning a state or national title or finding a cure for cancer, whatever it is you're talking about, the mentality of making the impossible possible is taught through what we do on a daily basis at practice. I think that is one of the most important reasons for the success we have had at Iowa."

"We continue to search for new truths and ideas to challenge our team. It's the pursuit of excellence that keeps us going. A musician wants each composition to improve on the last, an artist keeps wiping off the canvas until it has caught what his mind's eye wants to convey. Greatness starts in the mind."

GABLE USES WRESTLING AFFIRMATIONS

Gable has his wrestlers' repeat positive affirmations as a cornerstone of their mental-toughness training. I have used a similar technique in both baseball and MMA and have found it to be a successful form of mental-toughness conditioning. The following are brief lists of wrestling and baseball affirmations.

WRESTLING AFFIRMATIONS

- I can take down anyone at anytime
- Nobody can take me down
- No one can ride me
- No one can turn me
- I can ride and control anyone
- I can pin anyone

BASEBALL AFFIRMATIONS

- I am a strong and powerful pitcher
- I welcome adversity, it makes me stronger
- My hands are fast and I can turn on anything
- I see the ball deep and drive it the other way
- My defense is my strength, I love my glove

The athletes I work with select affirmations that are unique to them and their goals. We then write their affirmations on an index card and place it where it will be seen on a daily basis. I often suggest the bathroom mirror or the dashboard of their car.

Athletes have to condition their minds just like they condition their bodies. Consistent, daily repetition of the thoughts that we want our athletes to use when they are competing at the highest level are the thoughts that we must condition on a daily basis through the use of positive affirmations.

FINAL THOUGHTS

As I look over my pages of notes one more time, maybe Gable's most important message is his thoughts on what separates those who are champions vs. those who fall short.

"If you're going to be great in life or in sports, you must welcome competition, and great competition at that," Gable said. "Most people let their personal standards dominate them in times of difficulty and never press through the adversity to see how good they can be. Most people think that the champion is the person who is 99% perfect and everyone else is about 50% perfect. Actually it's more like 99.8% for the champion and 99.7% for those who fall short. There is a small difference between the two."

"There is a champion inside of everyone. Hard work, discipline, dedication, determination, and the love of competition and adversity are what must be taught on a daily basis to bring out the champion in the young people we coach. We worked hard to do that on a daily basis and that is what made us mentally tough and what made us deserve to win."

*"True champions **compete with themselves** to see how good they can be at everything they do from working harder than anyone else and **being willing to do the things that no one else wants to do.**"*

– Dan Gable

*"I wanted our athletes to feel like they deserved to win because they were the hardest-working group in the nation. **It is not enough to want to win.** Wanting to win gets you nowhere. Deserving to win by **pushing your physical and mental limits on a DAILY basis** is what makes champions."*

– Dan Gable

KEY POINTS FOR REVIEW:

- True champions compete with themselves to see just how good they can be at everything they do.

- The ultimate competition is with yourself to see just how good you can be.

- You cannot pursue excellence in one area of your life and fail to pursue it in every other aspect.

- Practices should be more physically and mentally challenging than games.

- Compete to win; don't compete not to lose.

Visit www.SoWhatNextPitch.com/EXTRAS
For BONUS Mental Conditioning Material &
FREE Peak Performance Training Tools

Chapter 8 | DEVELOPING TEAM CHEMISTRY AND CAPTAINS

Bill Currier Shares His Expensive Experience in Developing

Tight Team Chemistry and Credible Captains

Bill Currier became the head baseball coach at the University of Vermont in 1986, when he was just twenty-six years old, becoming one of the youngest coaches in the history of NCAA Division I Baseball. Currently the head baseball coach at Fairfield University, Coach Currier shares what he feels are the essentials of running a great baseball program and what advice he would give to young coaches.

LEADERSHIP STARTS AT THE TOP

A ship will sail in the direction that the captain determines is the correct course. A team will go in the direction that its head coach displays.

"Leadership starts at the top, with the head coach," Currier says. "The way you dress, the way you treat other people, your enthusiasm. Everything that you want from your players you have to be willing to give or they will not respect your leadership at the top."

"If I want to see how I look to my players, I need to spend some time in their locker room because I am a firm believer that the players will take on the traits that the head coach shows most often. If you are positive, your team will be positive. If you are up when you win, and down when you lose, regardless of how you worked the process, your team will follow suit. Their actions will directly reflect your example."

"Many of these young men are away from home for the first time and I have a duty as their coach to mentor them and show them how to act responsibly and be a contributing member of society. As coaches, it's our duty to teach our players about more than just the game of baseball. We need to be teaching them about the game of life as well."

ASSISTANT COACHES MUST BE AWARE OF INFLUENCE

In today's game, where the head coach can be pulled in a thousand different directions, it's often the assistant coaches who spend more time with the players, both on and off the field.

"Assistant coaches must understand that they are important representatives of the program and can often have a bigger influence on the development of the student-athlete than the head coach, and often more than anyone else at the university because of the time spent with the athlete," Currier says. "Assistant coaches must also be aware of their body language, their tone, and how they act, both on and off the field, because they are usually much closer in age to the players and have a more personal relationship with them."

"The assistant coach is a very important role, a role that you need to mentor and spend a lot of time advising if you are the head coach. Your assistants are out recruiting, they are very visible around campus, within the athletic department, and at camps. You must spend time teaching them what your program and personal philosophies are if you are going to be successful."

GOOD CAPTAINS CAN MAKE GOOD SEASONS

Often when captains are picked, it can become a popularity contest and the best leaders on your team don't always get appointed. Currier has had a lot of captains, and he says the differences between good and great captains are clear.

"Having great captains is a critical element of your team's leadership and is necessary if you are going to achieve the amount of success that your program is capable of," Currier says. "In my twenty-five-plus years of coaching, I can probably count on one hand the number of 'great' captains I have had."

"A great captain in my mind is a player who is going to put the success of the team over the importance of his friendship with his best friend or any individual on the team. I think too often captains try to be *liked* rather than try to do what is in the best interest of the long-term development of the program. There is nothing easy about being a great captain and leading your peers, especially during difficult times."

"Our greatest captains have been an extension of the coaching staff and had a great understanding of what direction the coaching staff wanted the program to go in, and how they could help assist us in taking the team in that direction."

GREAT PLAYERS NOT ALWAYS GREAT CAPTAINS

On many teams, the captain is also the star player or the player who has been on the team the longest. Currier finds that often his best captains are the kids who are the players that may not play the most, but are the most willing to put the team ahead of themselves.

"Our best captains have been ninth pitchers or the fourth catcher," Currier says. "They are the guys who show up every day and do whatever they can to help the team. They are not as concerned with their individual success as they are with team success."

"They are the guys who are genuinely interested in helping other players get better and who the freshmen gravitate towards for answers on how to succeed in college. They are generally the hardest-working guys on the team and at the top of the scale academically. *They are the guys who may not be the most popular, but are the most well-respected because of their attitude, work ethic, and desire to see others and the team succeed.*"

MENTORING PROGRAM A BIG SUCCESS

One way that Currier has tried to develop a team culture of success and a culture of doing things the right way has been through the establishment of a mentoring program.

"When our recruits come on campus is when the mentoring process starts," Currier says. "We try to pair the recruit up with a sophomore on campus who will be here if the recruit decides that our school is a place for him. That way we are establishing a positive contact for that incoming freshman before he arrives on campus. That mentorship extends into the weight room, study halls, and into practice. The upperclassman shows the underclassman what our standards of excellence are and what the right way to do things is."

"This has been great for us in getting freshmen to act like sophomores and to play like sophomores because they are more accustomed to the school and to our program. They have had someone there showing them the ropes and have not had to figure it all out on their own."

"I think this has done a lot for our program in establishing great relationships between the players, great team chemistry, and has helped us off the field to succeed in the classroom and to avoid a lot of the negative things that can happen on college teams, such as hazing or class-distinction issues."

TEAM RETREATS PAY BIG DIVIDENDS

Currier has also taken his teams on team retreats that he feels have done a lot for bringing his teams closer together.

"We have always participated in the Keith Cooper Memorial Run, a team run in memory of a former player, and do some community service projects, such as helping with a local Ronald McDonald House auction," Currier says. "We have in the past six years taken the team on an overnight campout where the players stay in lean-tos and cook dinner over a big bonfire. We have each class get up and do skits that range from re-enacting TV shows to poking fun at each other's mannerisms. It's one of the most fun nights of the year and really pulls us closer together. It also helps all of us understand the different personalities on the team."

"We have also participated in an annual wiffleball game at a local wiffleball stadium that is a miniature replica of Fenway Park. Our kids love playing there and it's a lot of fun. Since we have started to do more of these team retreats, I have seen off- the-field team chemistry and class relationships improve."

WHEN YOU STOP LEARNING, STOP COACHING

Currier shared what advice he would give to young coaches or people looking to improve their coaching abilities.

"I think the biggest thing is being a lifelong learner," Currier says. "Once you stop learning, it's time to stop coaching. Maybe it's a new way to teach a fundamental skill, or a different way to teach a skill from a more visual perspective and from less of an auditory approach."

"Every time I watch a game on TV or I'm at a high-school game recruiting, I'm always looking for new things, things that I think I can take back and use in my program."

"Attending the ABCA and your local state organization's clinic is another great way to learn and give back to the game."

Understanding the influence that captains, mentors, and team-building activities can have on your program is essential for success. Never underestimate how much of an impact you as a coach and your program can have on the total development of your players as people.

KEY POINTS FOR REVIEW:

• Leadership starts at the top with the head coach. A team often takes on the traits that the head coach displays most often.

• Coaches have a duty to teach their players about the game of life as well as the game of baseball.

• Head coaches must take the time to teach their assistants about personal and program philosophies.

• Great captains put the team's success ahead of friendships and their own individual success. They are often the most-respected players because of their attitude and work ethic.

• Mentoring programs and team retreats can build positive team chemistry.

Visit www.SoWhatNextPitch.com/EXTRAS
For BONUS Mental Conditioning Material &
FREE Peak Performance Training Tools

Chapter 9 | WINNING THE GAME
WITHIN THE GAME

Steve Trimper, head baseball coach at the University of Maine, is one of the brightest young coaches in the country. In his first season at the helm of the tradition-rich Black Bear program, Trimper led his team to the America East conference tournament championship and an NCAA Regional bid. Trimper shared some of his tips for success.

SURROUND YOURSELF WITH GREAT PEOPLE

Trimper attributes a lot of his success to having the opportunity to work with and play for some of the game's best coaches.

"I have been fortunate to be around great people," Trimper said. "I played for Bill Holowaty at Eastern Connecticut State University and he is one of the best in the business; an ABCA Hall of Famer and a great role model for players and coaches. I also had the opportunity to coach with Bill Currier at the University of Vermont and I think he is one of the best hitting coaches around."

"I got my first head coaching job at Manhattan College when I was twenty-seven years old and was able to develop my coaching skills. Bob Byrnes, our Athletic Director, was extremely supportive and worked hard to provide us with everything we needed to be successful. Surrounding yourself with great people not only helps speed up the learning process, but it also motivates you to be the best you can be day in and day out."

RECRUITING IS ABOUT MORE THAN JUST TOOLS

Trimper knows that the success of his coaching career is largely determined by the quality of student-athletes that he can get into the blue and black of a Maine baseball uniform. He has been able to recruit as well as anyone in the northeast, constantly getting top recruits to commit and play for the Black Bears.

"You have to get the players with the physical tools, but I also try to get in and pick their mind a little bit," Trimper said. "I try to find out what their social skills are like, what their families are like, and what their character is like. I really want to know how they handle failure. I like to see kids a few times in hope that I see them strike out or give up a walk-off homerun. I want to see their reaction to failure because at the Division I level everyone is going to taste failure at some point."

"We then bring the recruits on campus and try to surround them with the people in our program. That is critical because they get a good feeling for what we are all about, and our players are pretty good about getting a feel for what the recruit is like, and if he is the type of person we want in our family for the next four years."

STRESS THE POSITIVE

Trimper knows that if he is going to land a top recruit, he needs to spend all his time talking about the positives of his program. He does not waste time talking down other programs, which happens with some coaches in the recruiting process.

"We really try to stress the positives here at Maine," Trimper said. We really try to sell the positives about our program because that is what we can control. I cannot control what other schools can offer, or what other coaches say to their recruits about the University of Maine. All I can do is focus on that which I can control, which is promoting what I think makes Maine Baseball one of the best programs in the country for a kid to play for and develop in."

HONESTY & INTEGRITY WIN

Trimper knows that there are many different approaches to becoming a successful recruiter. He has found that the best way is the honest way.

"It's not about trying to pull the wool over kids' eyes or getting them to believe things that are not true," Trimper said. "You have to be honest, stress the positives, and also let them become aware of the areas of your school and program that need improvement. You have to treat that student-athlete like he is one of your own. You need to make a commitment to that person and his family and nothing should change when he shows up on campus. If it does, you were probably less than honest in the recruiting process."

"You have to help the recruit find the right fit for him and his family. Sometimes that may or may not be your school and that is okay. The recruits will often get a feeling when they are on campus that this is or is not a place for me, and they will usually get that feeling right away by the way you greet them as a coach and by the way the players interact with them. I usually get a call about twenty minutes after a recruit leaves campus saying that The University of Maine is the place for them, or not. It really should be that easy for a kid if we have done our job at being upfront and honest through the recruiting process."

TRIMPER USES PAST PLAYERS & PEERS FOR HELP

Trimper knows that he cannot physically get out and see all the great players in the country so he uses past players and peers in the game of baseball as filters for a prospective Black Bear.

"As I have said before, when you surround yourself with good people, good things happen. I constantly get calls from former players and peers such as Brian Cain and Ed Hockenbury who are willing to share with me some of the names of the top players in their areas," Trimper said. "If they call and give me a heads-up on a player, I am in my car that week to go see that player."

"It's all about developing positive relationships with people. That's not just on the baseball field, that's a life skill. I truly feel that when a person makes a commitment to come play for the Black Bears, it's my job not only to coach that person on the field but to be his mentor and teach him the skills that are necessary to succeed in life after baseball as well. I want our players to leave here with the confidence that they will do the best they can do in the first job interview they have."

GIVING ATHLETES THE OPPORTUNITY TO GROW

Often athletes personalize their performance and put too much pressure on themselves because they see themselves only as baseball players. Trimper knows that this trap is unhealthy and tries to put his players in situations where they can be successful and develop life skills off the field.

"I try to get our players out in the community, doing some form of public speaking," Trimper said. "I want them to be heavily involved with our camps for a variety of reasons. It's great for them to give back to our program and to the game of baseball, but, most importantly, it gives them an opportunity to teach and interact with the future of the game, the kids who come to Black Bear Baseball Camps."

"We try to give them a good experience, both on and off the field, so no matter what happens to them in the future, they will be confident and prepared."

EXPERIENCE AT DIVISIONS I, II, & III HELPS

Trimper, who started his playing career at Division II Elon College in North Carolina and then was a key part of a Division III National Championship team at Eastern Connecticut State University, has both playing and coaching experience at each level of college baseball.

"At the higher levels of each division, all those teams are good. If you change the Division III to a Division I, for a lot of those teams, they are still going to be very competitive. They have some great ball players," Trimper said. "I think there is a wide range of teams in each division. Having experience at each level has helped me understand how I can best help each kid, even if he decides he doesn't want to come to Maine. I've always felt that if I take the approach of trying to help a kid find the program that fits him best, the game will reward me and I will get the right guys to come to our program."

KEY POINTS FOR REVIEW:

- A coach should try to surround himself with great people.

- In recruiting, look for the players with physical tools that can also handle adversity.

- Spend your recruiting time stressing the positives of your own program rather than talking down your competition.

- Be honest and help the recruit find the best fit for him and his family.

- Develop positive relationships with people you trust to help identify potential recruits.

Visit www.SoWhatNextPitch.com/EXTRAS
For BONUS Mental Conditioning Material &
FREE Peak Performance Training Tools

Chapter 10 | MENTAL CONDITIONING WITH MOONLIGHT GRAHAM

Montana Coach Gives
Mental-Conditioning Tips

Johnny "Moonlight" Graham, is a successful American Legion baseball coach from Belgrade, Montana and has a unique coaching situation. Unlike most states, Montana high schools do not offer baseball. The brand of baseball that most Montana high-school-age players participate in is summer American Legion.

Operating under American Legion policies and procedures and not those of the National Federation of High Schools or the Montana High School Association provides the coach with an interesting situation. The high school educational-based ideal of "teaching life lessons through sports" could easily be lost amidst the sixty-plus-game schedule and isolation from athletic directors and academic standards.

Coach Graham, also a seventh-grade social-studies teacher and athletic director, has found a successful approach to educating young men through a character and process-based approach to coaching baseball.

"I hold my players to the highest standards," Graham said. "When they are out of school in the summer, a lot of players will have the tendency to lose focus and take advantage of the summer while letting their baseball development and career slip right through their hands. *We truly believe that it's not how many days you put in but what you put into those days that really count.*"

ONE DAY AT A TIME

Graham takes pride in developing a *"don't count the days, make the days count"* mentality in his players. His players, in turn, find that focusing on one day at a time allows them to better manage the stress and time demands of the long season.

"In baseball it can become very easy for you to start counting the days until your first game or your last game, conference play, or playoffs," Graham said. "We really work at developing a mentality from coaches and players that it is not about the number of days, but what we put into those days that counts. *We really take a quality-over-quantity approach.*"

Joel Barnett, who has played the last three seasons for Graham, echoed the coach's sentiments.

"It's funny because Coach Graham is always challenging us to see how good we can be today. What are we working on today?" Barnett said. "As players we take a similar approach to school and life in general. Take it one day at a time, focus on the process and do the best work you can. Overall, just try to *control what you can control, your attitude, your preparation and your effort.*"

HAVE TO vs. WANT TO MENTALITY

Graham and his assistants, Brandon Steadman and Mark Bolin, also created a unique philosophy in which players were able to use self-talk to help turn around their practices, games, at-bats, and performances.

"We used Brian Cain's PRIDE program and one of the things that we took away from it was that we WANT to play baseball every day in the summer, not that we HAVE to play baseball every day in the summer," Graham said. "It was Augie Garrido from the University of Texas who said that your two chief opponents in baseball are frustration and boredom."

"I'm sure that if Coach Garrido is dealing with that at his level, we are dealing with that a lot more here because there isn't the school affiliation or large crowds that can keep you motivated. We decided as a program that we would really emphasize that today we WANT to play or today we WANT to practice rather than we HAVE to. This mentality makes a significant difference because when you take an approach of WANT to vs. HAVE to you start to appreciate the game and love the grind and the challenges that it presents. You also realize the opportunity that you have to play this great game."

"There is that little battle we all fight inside of our own heads, and if we give into the HAVE to and the drudgery rather than focus on the process and getting 1% better every day, *the game can really beat you up. It's designed that way and you have to play the game the right way, both physically and mentally, to be successful.*"

PROCESS vs. OUTCOME APPROACH

Graham has found that stressing the process, as opposed to the outcome or end result, and teaching how to play the game the right way (one pitch at a time, in the present moment, focused on the process with a positive mentality) is the best means necessary to give yourself the best chance to obtain your desired outcome of winning. This approach has helped his players to relax, play better, and enjoy the challenges the game has to offer.

"There are so many things in baseball that you cannot control and so many things that happen to make it a game of failure that *if you get stuck on evaluating your success solely on results, you are going to get burned out very fast because YOU CAN'T control results in this game*," Graham said. "That is one of the biggest adjustments we have to make mentally with our players when they come out for the team."

"I think we have had success relating the process-over-outcome approach to our players and how that works outside of baseball as well. There are so many things in life that you can't control, family, weather, injury, etc., that you can get hooked on and pulled into a negative spiral very quickly."

"As a member of our program, coach or player, you understand that there is a complete and total commitment to the process and to doing everything you can on a daily basis to give yourself and the team the best chance for success. To us, that is not an approach that is about winning, it's much more than that. It's about excellence. We hope that our players take that same mentality into life after they're done playing."

KEY POINTS FOR REVIEW:

- It's not how many days you put in, but what you put into the days that really count.

- Control what you can control; your attitude, your preparation and your effort.

- The game of baseball can really beat you up. It's designed that way and you have to play the game the right way, both physically and mentally, to be successful.

- If you get stuck evaluating your success solely on results, you are going to get burned out fast because you cannot control the results.

Visit www.SoWhatNextPitch.com/EXTRAS
For BONUS Mental Conditioning Material &
FREE Peak Performance Training Tools

Chapter 11 | FIGHTING A BATTLE MUCH TOUGHER THAN BASEBALL

Casey O'Rourke Discusses

How Cancer Took Away His Ability to Play the Game,

But Exposed New Lessons He Never Would Have Learned

Casey O'Rourke was coming off the best summer season of his life. He was 11-1 for the Thunder Bay Border Cats of the Northwoods Summer Collegiate Baseball League, started the league's all-star game, and was looking forward to his junior season at the University of Iowa. Head coach Jack Dahm had penciled him in as the club's ace pitcher and expected him to be a draft choice by Major League Baseball at the season's end.

A constant, sharp, nagging pain in O'Rourke's abdomen and testicle, multiple misdiagnoses, and an appendix removal surgery led O'Rourke back to the doctor's office on December 8, 2005, for what he thought would be another routine appointment.

Several hours later that day he was facing one of life's toughest opponents.

The 21 year-old was diagnosed with testicular cancer.

"I remember getting the call from Casey while I was sitting in my office," Coach Dahm said. "I picked up the phone expecting him to tell me that he was going to be late to practice or that he has to take a final exam and Casey says, 'Coach, I got it.' Not knowing what to do or what to say, I just drove to the hospital so I could be there with Casey. It was the most difficult day of my coaching career."

It was Stage Two testicular cancer. The disease had polluted one testicle and had moved on to his lymph nodes. Multiple surgeries and weeks of chemotherapy lay ahead.

Later that night, the Iowa baseball team met for the last time before Christmas break. Teammates who had called O'Rourke throughout the day were getting worried. He wasn't answering.

"I started the meeting and was going to break the news to the team and in walked Casey with his father," Coach Dahm said.

"That was one of the toughest times I've ever had, telling the team," O'Rourke said. "I was walking in there, seeing the guys. None of them knew. I couldn't tell them."

So Dahm told the team. Baseball was already hard enough to think about in the midst of a snow storm, and it inched further back in the players' minds when they heard the news about their beloved teammate.

"It was neat to see all the guys right after the meeting gather with Casey and be supportive," Coach Dahm recalled. "But man, that was hard on everyone."

Just over two years removed from the diagnosis, O'Rourke was cleared of cancer. After trying to make a comeback on the mound for the Hawkeyes during the spring of 2007, the once- dominant right-hander found that the wear and tear his body had endured fighting cancer was just too much to overcome to perform at the professional level.

As a fifth-year senior at Iowa and the program's student assistant, O'Rourke created a new mission in life: He wanted to educate people around the country about testicular cancer in hopes that he can give back, not only to the game of baseball, but to the game of life. In this chapter, O'Rourke discusses some of the life lessons he learned through overcoming the toughest challenge of his life.

FRUSTRATION/IMMATURITY ALMOST LED TO TRANSFER

O'Rourke's Iowa pitching career wasn't laden with the success that he experienced in the Northwoods League. After his sophomore season he almost decided to transfer or step away from the game completely.

"I remember that summer of '05, in the Northwoods League, wanting to transfer from Iowa or just get away from the game completely," O'Rourke said. "I was putting a lot of pressure on myself and was not communicating with my coaches. I was miserable and it was my own fault. I felt like I was owed something and didn't even know what it was. I grew up a lot that summer and realized that Iowa was the place for me. In retrospect, having been through what I have with cancer, I know now that staying at Iowa was the best thing I ever did."

"When you are young and new to the college scene, it can be overwhelming at times. Having cancer really changes your perspective and makes you look at things differently. I used to make big deals out of everything, way bigger than they needed to be. I think people who can learn to keep it simple and to focus on things that they can control are the ones who are able to play their best and have the most fun. That summer in Thunder Bay *I quit caring about what other people were going to think, or what other people were going to say, and I just went out and pitched my game.*"

THE ULTIMATE TEST OF A COMPETITOR'S SPIRIT

One of the hardest things that O'Rourke had to deal with was chemotherapy. At times, he found both the physical and psychological battles unbearable.

"I think the chemo was the hardest thing I have ever had to deal with, both physically and psychologically," O'Rourke said. "I was sick and sore all the time, but the hardest part was having my two younger brothers come in and see me weak. Being from a small town where you are the only Division I athlete that has ever come from your high school, where everyone has such high expectations for you and you have such high expectations for yourself, to have something like that put on you was not easy to handle."

PATIENCE IS A VIRTUE

In a sport where there is no clock, great baseball players and coaches understand that having patience is a critical part of the game. O'Rourke feels that one of the things he learned through his battle with cancer that he hopes to pass on to others is the importance of having patience.

"I never had patience before I had cancer," O'Rourke said. "I learned that having patience is essential in life, just as it is in baseball. In baseball you try to figure things out and fix them quickly. But there are times when things just don't come quickly. You have to be able to accept that and keep moving forward one day at a time with a positive attitude or you're going to beat yourself up mentally to the point where you lose all motivation."

WORKING SMARTER – NOT LONGER

If you had a headache and were prescribed two Advil, you would not take twenty and expect the pain to go away ten times faster. In baseball, however, many people take the approach that working longer and harder will yield quicker results. That is not always the case.

"My body did not react well to the treatments and I tried to push myself, thinking I would recover more quickly," O'Rourke said. "I had been in bed for six months and I wanted to start working as hard as I could to get back on the hill, but I would take one step forward and two steps back until I learned to trust my doctors and follow their rehab program. Working harder does not always mean you are working smarter and are going to get better. I think a lot of players, especially those who get injured, could learn a lot from my experience and I hope that my expensive experience provides them with inexpensive experience."

CANCER DOES NOT CARE ABOUT TIME – MAKE THE MOST OF YOURS

After defeating cancer, Lance Armstrong, one of the most famous cancer survivors, took over two years off before he went on to dominate the Tour de France. Unfortunately for O'Rourke, the NCAA has time restrictions on the number of years you have to compete, and one of his major goals was to get back on the mound for the Hawkeyes during the 2007 season.

"I came back, started working out and felt great, but the recovery time afterwards was much, much longer than I expected," O'Rourke said. "It was difficult, but just to be able to be out there and get on the mound, and to be with the guys again was one of the best feelings I have ever had. It was right up there with when doctors told me I was cancer-free. I had a new-found admiration for the game and didn't beat myself up when I threw a bad pitch or had a bad outing. I have never enjoyed the game as much as I did when I came back after cancer. I can't believe I took those first years of college ball for granted."

DON'T COUNT THE DAYS, MAKE THE DAYS COUNT

The commitment to get the most out of each and every day is a common trait among peak performers and people who get the most out of their ability. Baseball players, however, all too often start counting the days until their next game, wasting all the days of preparation and development that come with quality practice.

"During my freshman and sophomore years I would cross off the days of practice until it was game day," O'Rourke said. "I dreaded going to practice, as I think a lot of college baseball players around the country do. I was totally counting the days."

"When I was done with cancer and I could play again, everything had changed. I couldn't wait to be at practice and push myself to the point where I would vomit from exhaustion, and then get up and do some more. It was a totally different perspective. I wanted to see how hard I could go and how good I could be on a daily basis."

"Any college or high-school player is fortunate to be able to put on a uniform each and every day. Don't take it for granted. Learn from each and every day and constantly come back to what you love about the game. I think I learned to look at the game with a deeper perspective and learned to really appreciate and enjoy the game more."

CONTROL WHAT YOU CAN CONTROL

Coming from a game where you have very little control over the results, O'Rourke understood that defeating cancer, just like playing baseball, was *more about the process than about the result*. Success came down to doing what you needed to do on a daily basis to give yourself the best chance to get your desired end result.

"I really learned to control what I could control," O'Rourke said. "I could take the medicine, I could control what I thought and said to myself. I also came to realize that when I was out there on the mound, I could not always control how I felt, but could control what I thought, and how I assessed certain situations. I never thought that way before cancer, and when I came back to pitch in 2007, I was much more at ease and comfortable on the mound. I wish I had figured all that out before, when I was physically able to pitch."

EMBRACING FAILURE BY STAYING POSITIVE

In a sport in which you are considered one of the elite if you succeed 30-35%% of the time, learning to handle failure and stay positive are as essential as the physical skills needed to play the game. But staying positive in the face of adversity can be difficult. Without fear there is no courage.

"It's hard to stay positive when you're not getting the results you want, but you have to stay positive if you want to play well on a consistent basis," O'Rourke said. "You have to remember that it's only a game, and a game where you can't control the result, a game that is extremely difficult mentally, and a game of failure. If baseball were easy, everyone would be playing it. You have to learn to embrace failure by staying positive."

FOCUS ON SMALL VICTORIES

Motivation can come from setting and achieving small daily goals. For O'Rourke, setting daily goals and finding small victories was essential to fuel his fire to keep fighting and see the light at the end of a dark and dismal tunnel.

"Looking for small improvements is a great way to stay motivated," O'Rourke said. "I was always looking for the big improvements and big gains and once I was able to come back from cancer and focus on the small improvements, those were the things that gave me the most enjoyment and the most motivation. I think the small improvements are always there, even when you have been healthy your entire career. I just think we often get caught in a cycle where we forget to look for the small victories in life."

WORST THING BECOMES BEST THING – KEEP HOPE

The mythical story of the Phoenix rising from the ashes to find a new beginning has provided hope for people faced with difficulty and loss for ages. Often it is out of our darkest days that the brightest lights begin to shine.

"I think towards the end of treatment I started to learn that sometimes the worst things that happen to you can become the best things if you choose to make them that way," O'Rourke said. "Just like with anything, you become close to the people who you spend time with and are trying to help you. I learned the importance of being human and being willing to spend time with others, and to give back."

"I want to be that guy who can say he had testicular cancer. I want to be that guy who can provide a glimmer of hope to people out there who get diagnosed and can use a little inspiration or pick-me-up. For me *hope is an acronym for Hold On, Possibilities Exist and Hear Other People's Experiences.* My mission is to help people keep a positive mindset by seeing all the possibilities that still lie ahead of them. Hopefully, I can do that through sharing my experiences."

"If I can help one person overcome a battle with chemotherapy or cancer, then I have had a successful life. Cancer has given me a newly found appreciation for the simpler things in life and for everyday blessings and successes. I want to share that appreciation."

LEARNING TO LEAD

Sometimes you don't choose to be a leader, but being a leader chooses you. For O'Rourke, wasting time feeling sorry for himself was not an option. The only option was to make a difference and to embrace being a leader in his community.

"The week that Casey found out he was diagnosed with testicular cancer, I asked him whether he wanted it to become public," Coach Dahm said. "He did, so we made an announcement and Channel 7 came to do an interview with him. I think Casey learned a lot that first week because his interview aired and a few days later he was walking into the hospital and found out that two people who had seen his interview had come in for exams and found out they too had testicular cancer."

"I think that was something that really helped Casey. I think he learned that by telling his story, it might help save someone else's life. From that point on, I think Casey really opened up and grew as a person. He embraced more of a leadership role."

"I was never a vocal leader when I was a player in high school or college," O'Rourke said. "I was put in a position where I had to lead. When I sat down and thought about it, I realized that I did have what it took to be a leader, that I did have the knowledge and the experience. Sometimes you get put into situations and you don't realize you are in that situation at the moment, but you learn to communicate better, you learn to like the smiles on people's faces a lot more, and you learn to lead."

"You don't know where your life is going to take you. You don't know when that moment is going to come in your life that defines you. I didn't know my moment was coming when it came. When you get that moment, and you feel that moment, run with it."

DISCOVERING A PURER FORM OF SUCCESS

After his fight with cancer, O'Rourke rediscovered his love for the game of baseball. Moving beyond outcome oriented success, O'Rourke began to measure the success of his performances on a purer scale. His newfound appreciation for life and baseball enabled him to better ignore that which was outside of his control and provided him enhanced focus on the daily processes in his personal drive for excellence.

"You can succeed. Anyone can succeed if they believe it in their heart and can visualize it in their mind. Have a positive attitude, don't feel sorry for yourself, and don't take your frustrations out on anyone but yourself because they are what you make them."

"I could not control cancer, but I could control how I felt, how I thought, and how I would react mentally. Take it the right way, be a leader, be positive, and move on. I see too many people who are negative all the time and it has to be a miserable way to live. You can choose to see the positives or you can choose to see the negatives. Your perspective is your choice."

"Life is all about moving on. Fortunately, I have learned that at a young age. I hope I never have to learn it again. I hope that everyone can find small victories and build a foundation on which to grow."

Casey's mother, Susie, said it best. "As a parent of a pitcher, you sit in the stands, and every pitch, you worry. Is it a strike? Is it a ball? Well, when I got to see him pitch after cancer, I didn't give a crap where the ball went. I was happy just to see him pitch."

OUTSTANDING OPPORTUNITY FOR YOU

Any coach looking to provide an opportunity for his team that will inspire, motivate, educate and have lasting impact, please feel free to contact Casey O'Rourke to discuss having him come speak in your community or to your team, or set up a Skype session in which he can share his inexpensive experience with your team.

"Testicular cancer is something that is not talked about a lot and it needs to be. I am wide-open to sharing my story and giving back to the baseball community that has given me so much. I would love to talk with students about cancer and about overcoming hardships in life. I can be reached by e-mail at orourke32@gmail.com or give me a call at (319) 530-8320."

KEY POINTS FOR REVIEW:

- **Patience is important in baseball and in life; you need to move forward one day at a time with a positive attitude or you could lose your motivation.**

- **Motivation can come from setting small daily goals and achieving them.**

- **Instead of counting the days until the next game, make the days count by preparing and improving.**

- **Handling adversity and staying positive are as important in baseball as physical skills like throwing and hitting.**

Visit www.SoWhatNextPitch.com/EXTRAS
For BONUS Mental Conditioning Material &
FREE Peak Performance Training Tools

Chapter 12 | THE MENTALITY
NO HITTER WANTS TO FACE

Glenn Swanson Breaks Down
Mentality of Firing First No-Hitter

When a pitcher does something spectacular, such as throwing a no-hitter, some coaches will say, "He played over his head." What does that mean? That the pitcher got lucky? The other team had a bad day? A combination of both?

From a mental-game perspective, what happens is that the pitcher gets totally engrossed in the moment, playing one pitch at a time, with an emphasis on the process and on what he can control, with a positive mentality. This heightened awareness and peak-performance pitching mentality is something that happens less than 10% of the time, but it's something that can happen more often with mental conditioning. I feel that mental conditioning coaches often make the mistake of spending too much time talking about the zone and not enough time talking about how to stay in the battle when you don't have your best stuff.

When pitchers try to recreate success – when they go out and try to out do what they did in their last performance – they are not playing one pitch at a time. They have too much of their attention on the past.

I often tell players, "If what you did yesterday looks big, than you have not done anything today." When you have a great outing, enjoy it, savor it, but make a commitment that at a specific time you will put that outing to rest and start to focus on your next outing.

Going out to the mound to protect your no-hitter or to save a lead is one of the worst mentalities you can take to the hill. It causes you to be passive and perform at less than your best.

There are two types of pitchers, those who compete to win and those who play not to lose. I will bet the farm on the guy going all-out, taking risks, making pitches and pitching with the mindset to win rather than pitching not to lose.

The best way to come back and pitch after a great outing is to focus on your next pitch. The best way to come back after a bad outing is to focus on the next pitch. Baseball is a simple game; people are complex.

FOCUS ON FUNCTION NOT FEEL

Glenn Swanson of the University of California, Irvine, didn't try to do anything differently when he took the mound on April 25, 2006, for a Tuesday spot-start against the University of San Diego. As a matter of fact, he didn't feel all that good to begin with.

"I had actually been sick for about a week," the crafty left handed pitcher said. "I didn't feel all that great before the game, either, but once I put my spikes on, that all goes out the window. The only things I think about are pounding the zone and trying to find a way to help the team win."

On that day, Swanson did more than help find a way to win; he pitched the game of his life, a nine-inning no-hitter with 14 strikeouts and only one walk on only 89 pitches, leading the Anteaters to a 7-0 win.

"I didn't try to do anything special. I just stuck to my routine and kept the good thoughts going. I knew that if I could continually pound the zone, we would have the best chance of winning the game. I just stuck to my routine, my deep breath before each pitch, and used my cue words before each pitch, just like our mental conditioning coach Brian Cain had worked with us on. I was totally focused on taking it one pitch at a time and we got the desired end result."

Coming off a Big West Conference loss three days earlier to UC Santa Barbara in which Swanson entered the game in the ninth inning with the lead, Coach Dave Serrano was just looking for his fifth-year senior to get in some innings before turning the game over to the rest of the Anteaters staff.

"My intention was to have Swanny go for three or four innings," Serrano said. "His pitch count was low and he was throwing strikes so we stuck with him. Swanny is one of the hardest- working guys I have had the privilege of coaching. He has had to overcome a lot of adversity in his five years here at UCI. I don't know if I have ever seen a team pull for a guy like we do for him. That's because he's such a great teammate, and the guys all have great respect and admiration for him."

Swanson, who had strung together fourteen hitless innings over two starts, retired the first five batters in a start the following Sunday against UC Davis before giving up a hit in the second inning. He managed to hold the Aggies scoreless until the fifth when they finally pushed across a run, ending his stretch of scoreless innings at 17.2.

"I've been going out there and just pitching my game," Swanson said. "It doesn't matter who's in the box, who we're playing, what the score is, or the magnitude of the game. My job as a pitcher is to pound the mitt. That's all I can control. Once the ball leaves my hand, I can't control what happens, if the umpire makes a bad call, if I give up a hit, or if a teammate makes an error. If I pound the mitt consistently, I am giving myself and the team the best chance for success, and that is all I can do. Working with our mental conditioning coach and coming to grips with this understanding that I have to control what I can control and let everything else take care of itself has really helped me."

BACK-TO-BACK NATIONAL PLAYERS OF THE WEEK

Swanson's teammate Justin Cassel, a junior right-handed pitcher, was named Big West Pitcher of The Week and Collegiate Baseball "Louisville Slugger" National Player of The Week for his career-high fifteen strikeouts in 8.2 innings in a win over UC Santa Barbara on Friday, April 21, 2006. Swanson was named Big West Pitcher of The Week and Collegiate Baseball "Louisville Slugger" National Player of The Week the following week for his no-hit performance.

"This is the first time I can remember that two pitchers from the same staff have been named Collegiate Baseball 'Louisville Slugger' National Players of The Week in consecutive weeks," Serrano said. "We work really hard on getting our guys to play one pitch at a time, focused on the process, in the present moment, with a positive mentality, and both Justin and Swanny have worked closely with our mental conditioning coach to be able to do that better this season. They have both worked extremely hard, both physically and on their mental game. I think that attributes a lot to why they have been able to have this type of success."

VERBAL PITCH CUES LEAD TO CONSISTENCY

Swanson attributed his success to the consistency of his mechanics and also to the consistency of his thought process and mental game.

"*I have a verbal cue or pitch thought that I use for every pitch I throw.* If I am throwing a fastball in, I will say to myself, 'Pound it, pound it' over and over again so that nothing else can creep into my mind. Having this pitch thought or final thought acts as a mental filter and allows me to be aware of any other non-productive thoughts that might creep into my mind, such as a person in the stands or in the other dugout who is saying something, or if I start to get some self-doubt about my commitment to that pitch or any of the other thousand reasons why your mind can wander. When that happens, I just step off and re-set the process all over again."

"When I'm throwing a change-up, I will tell myself to 'extend, extend,' or on a curveball I might say 'pull it, pull it.' These pitch thoughts will change throughout the season, but I always say something to myself that will help me solidify my commitment to that pitch, and help give me the best chance to be successful."

ROUTINE DEEP BREATH HELPS KEEP GAME SIMPLE

One of the things that Swanson has done to help keep the game simple, and play it one pitch at a time, is develop a pre-pitch routine that he goes through before every pitch.

"One of the things I've worked on a lot this year is my routine. *Having a routine that you go through from the time the ball hits the catcher's mitt until it leaves your hand for the next pitch is critical for consistency and optimal performance.* I've always had a routine, but this year I've worked a lot more on it in the bullpen. In our mental conditioning program, we talk about increasing the quality of practice and the quality of our bullpens by working on our routine and pitching at the same pace and with the same mentality as we would in a game. I've really bought into that and it has helped keep the game simple for me because nothing changes, whether I'm in the pen or on in a game."

"Taking a good, deep breath before I pitch helps me relax and stay in control of myself. It also helps me stay in the present moment, and it makes each pitch the same because my routine is the same. The eighty-ninth pitch and the first pitch against San Diego were to the same location, with the same mechanics, with the same mindset. Nothing changes."

INJURY HELPED BUILD MENTAL TOUGHNESS

Swanson sat out the entire 2005 season with an injury and said that having a year off from pitching gave him a new perspective on playing the game.

"When I was injured, I really got into the mental game because I couldn't throw and I wanted to do something to get better. I read **Heads-Up Baseball** and spent a lot of time imaging myself pitching, and working on my routine.

Most importantly, it helped me take a new perspective on the game. I used to put a lot of pressure on myself to pitch well. If I didn't throw well, I would beat myself up for days. Now I have a much different perspective. I enjoy every day that I get to be out there because I have had that enjoyment, which we too often take for granted, taken away from me. I have a lot more fun and feel a lot less pressure, so I'm able to perform better."

LACE IT UP AND LOCK IT IN

Not to be confused with former Air Jordan spokesman Mars Blackman, Swanson mentioned that "it's all about the shoes."

"I'll show up to the field in my turf shoes and mess around with the guys and have fun. You can't be serious all the time in this game or you'll go crazy, there's just too much time. When it's time for me to get clicked in and start my game preparation, I lace up my spikes good and tight. That tightening of the laces is my cue that it's go-time. I use that tying of the spikes to get me checked into my ideal pitching mentality."

"After the game I will evaluate my performance, look at what I did well and what I could have done better. I try to learn from every outing. When I'm ready to be done with that day's performance, however, I take off my spikes, bang them together to get the dirt out, and let myself know that the day is over, and I'm making a commitment to move on, and let that day go, regardless of how good or bad I did. Whether I just threw the no-hitter or got rocked, when I take off the spikes, it's over. In baseball you have to turn the page. You play every day, and if you're not in the present moment, you soon will be history."

"In baseball you have to take it one day and one pitch at a time. You have to keep your highs low and your lows high. This is something that I have heard coaches say for a long time, but through working with our mental conditioning program with Coach Cain and Coach Serrano, I am finally figuring out how to actually 'let it go' and get to the next pitch, or the next day. This learning process has made the game a whole lot easier, and gets rid of a lot of the pressure I would put on myself."

ANTEATERS CLEAR THE FIELD

One of the things that Swanson and the rest of the Anteater pitching staff have done is challenge themselves to see how quickly they can breakdown the batting practice set-up after the visiting team hits at Anteater Ballpark. What started out as a joke has turned into a team-building exercise, which is now just as important to the preparation process as batting practice itself.

"One day we decided to see how quickly we could clean off the field after the visiting team took BP (Batting Practice)," Swanson said. "It took us about two minutes. It was funny but guys started strategizing on ways that they could clean the field quicker, and coming up with plans of who would do what and in what order things had to come off the field to get it done the quickest. As the season went on, our goal was to get it under a minute, then under forty-five seconds, then under forty seconds. As of now our record time is 36.96 seconds. Our goal is to keep getting better, just like we try to do every day on the field. If we keep getting better, we know that the desired end result will take care of itself."

"It really is an amazing deal to watch," Coach Serrano said. "Every pitcher knows exactly what he has to do. They all have to commit to their plan, stay within themselves, and give a best effort without trying too hard. All the things they need to do as a staff to beat their time in clearing the field is similar to the things they need to do on the mound to be successful. The guys have a lot of fun with it and I truly think that it has become part of the preparation process just like BP and infield. For our pitchers, clearing the field with a quality, game-like effort has become their BP. We want them to play with a relentless energy and this has become part of our system in the way we do things."

KEY POINTS FOR REVIEW:

• Verbal cues or pitch thoughts, such as "pound it," "extend," or "pull it," can solidify commitment to a pitch and prevent non-productive thoughts from creeping in.

• Follow the same routine in practice as you do in the game.

• Taking a good, deep breath before each pitch helps you feel relaxed and in control.

• Lacing up your spikes and locking in your focus can be a part of your routine and a sign that it's time to check into your pitching mentality.

• Taking off your spikes and pounding out the dirt can be a part of your routine and a sign that the game is over and it's time to move on, regardless of how you did.

Visit www.SoWhatNextPitch.com/EXTRAS
For BONUS Mental Conditioning Material &
FREE Peak Performance Training Tools

Chapter 13 | HITTING SUCCESS AND FAILURE IN CAPE COD

Cape League All-Star Matt Cusick
Shares Mental Tips for Turnaround

U niversity of Southern California infielder Matt Cusick '08 emerged as one of the top left-handed hitters in the country over his career as a Trojan Baseball player. *Cusick attributes some of his success to working hard, but he attributes the majority of his success to working smart.*

"I have worked a lot on my mental game," Cusick said. "My whole perspective on what it means to be successful at the plate has changed in the last few years. I fell into the results trap when I was in high school and you can't do that in college, especially at USC. The competition is so good; *you really have to focus on having quality at-bats and controlling what you can control.* You do that and everything else, the results, will take care of itself."

Cusick was one of the top hitters in college baseball. As a freshman in 2005, he started all 62 games and became the first freshman to hit leadoff on opening day for USC since Wes Rachels did it ten years prior. Cusick received all Pac-10 honors while hitting .311-4-35 and saving his best performance for the big stage, taking home NCAA Regional MVP Honors for his .750 (9-for-12) performance in Long Beach, California.

SUPER SOPHOMORE SEASON

A third baseman who doesn't hit for power, a leadoff man who doesn't steal a ton of bases, Cusick's list of shortcomings is a motivator that fuels his tremendous work ethic in the off-season. That work ethic helped him follow up his rookie season in 2006 by leading the Trojans at the plate, hitting .369-4-35.

"His success is a tribute to his work ethic and his passion and love for hitting," hitting coach Andy Nieto said in an article that appeared in the *USC Daily Trojan*. "He's a blue-collar guy when it comes to hitting; there can never be enough swings for him."

STRUGGLES ON CAPE COD

Cusick followed his super sophomore season by struggling in his first few weeks in the prestigious Cape Cod Baseball League. His strong mental make-up, however, allowed him to have one of the best turnarounds the highly competitive summer league has ever seen.

Cusick started down the slippery slope by going hitless in his first ten at-bats, one for his first eighteen, and three for his first thirty. Those were numbers that he was not accustomed to having.

"About a week, week and a half into the season, it was pretty rough," he remembered. "I was hitting balls hard, but they were right at people. I just couldn't get anything to drop. I got frustrated because I squared up some balls but had nothing to show for it. But that's baseball. *I knew I had to stick to my routine and control what I could control, which was having quality at-bats and trying to make solid contact.*"

BACKGROUND IN MENTAL CONDITIONING PAYS OFF

Cusick, who had taken Sport Psychology courses at USC, knew that many great hitters in college baseball have had similar early struggles on the Cape and have let those struggles snowball into horrible summers by overanalyzing and focusing too much on the end result.

"I tried to stay positive, I spoke to my coaches, and made one slight adjustment, moving my hands a little further from my body," Cusick said. "But the main thing was just staying positive, learning from each at-bat, getting better every day, and controlling what I can control. Seeing the ball well and taking good swings. I was able to stick to my mental conditioning program and focus on hitting the ball hard."

"Every day I would battle and the game started rewarding me. I would hit a ball hard to the shortstop and it would take a funny hop and get through for a base hit. Baseball is funny like that. *The harder you work and the better your preparation, the more luck you're going to have.* I hit some balls hard that were caught and I hit some balls that probably should have been outs that fell in for hits. *The game knows and rewards those who trust their approach and don't try to change things whenever they go 0-for-4 or have a bad day.*"

JOURNAL-KEEPING HELPS WITH PREPARATION

Cusick also attributes his hitting success largely to his off-field preparation. He would spend time each night writing in his hitting journal so he could have the confidence that he did everything he could possibly do to be successful.

"When I got home at night, I got on my laptop and wrote about each at-bat. The pitcher I saw, what types of pitches I faced, and any information that I think could help me in the future."

"In the morning, if I'm struggling, I will look back to times when I was struggling and see what I can pick out that I might be able to do to help me turn it around. I look at days when I was hitting well and read what my thoughts and self-talk were and duplicate them. I can see distinct differences in my journal entries from when I'm hitting the ball well to when I'm struggling. *The journal is a great way for me to look back at guys I have faced, and a way for me to feel totally prepared when I get in the box.*"

MENTAL IMAGERY HELPS SET STAGE FOR SUCCESS

Cusick also uses imagery as part of his daily and nightly preparation, a skill that many hitters often overlook.

"I use imagery as part of my preparation. It does not have to be a long process. I go through the different pitches that each guy threw me and replay my at-bats and get a clear view in my mind of what I did well, and replay what I can do better. For example, if a coach gave me a sign and I didn't execute, I will replay that at-bat and see myself executing like I want to. It helps with confidence and it helps with preparation."

WITNESSES OTHER HITTERS STRUGGLE

Cusick was able to turn his summer around and wound up being the fourth-best hitter on the Cape, hitting .304-2-12 and earning Cape Cod League All-Star status. But he saw many hitters who were not as well-versed in the mental game continue to give away at-bats and struggle against the best competition in the country.

"Everyone in the Cape is an all-star," Cusick said. "Everyone there is coming off of a .350 season with 10 homeruns, but the Cape is a different level. I read an article by Brian Cain that was in *Collegiate Baseball* in 2002 and he talked about how everyone wants to hit .300, but what they fail to realize is that very few hitters actually do. *When you evaluate your success solely on numbers, you can put way too much pressure on yourself because you can't control numbers; all you can control is having quality at-bats.*"

"I saw some guys who couldn't get away from looking at their average and focus on hitting the ball hard. A lot of guys struggled the first week like I did and they weren't able to get out of it. I think some of them threw in the towel and said, 'This league is way too good.' They let the self-doubt creep in because they were too concerned with numbers. I think a lot of guys there could have really benefitted from a mental conditioning program."

MENTAL CONDITIONING UNDER-USED

Cusick found that many of the players had little or no background in conditioning or sport psychology. He feels that mental conditioning is as big a part of his success as anything else.

"The Mental Game is the most important part of athletics, especially baseball, because it's such a game of failure. If you're working on the physical aspect on the field, taking ground balls, hitting in the cage, etc., and you're not working on the mental part, you're wasting your time. You can do everything right and still get out, and when you think about it that way, it's just absurd not to have any mental plan or mental conditioning system that helps you evaluate your success on factors that are within your control."

KEY POINTS FOR REVIEW:

• The harder you work and the better your preparation, the more luck you're going to have.

• The game knows and rewards those who trust their approach and don't try to change things whenever they go 0-for-4 or have a bad day.

• Stick to a routine and control what you can control, which was having quality at-bats and trying to make solid contact.

• Keeping a journal is a great way to look back at previous performances, and a way to feel totally prepared when you get in the box.

• When you evaluate your success solely on numbers, you can put way too much pressure on yourself because you can't control numbers. All you can control is having quality at-bats.

Visit www.SoWhatNextPitch.com/EXTRAS
For BONUS Mental Conditioning Material &
FREE Peak Performance Training Tools

Chapter 14 | UNC WILMINGTON MAKES THE MOST OF MENTAL CONDITIONING

Coaching Staff Places Heavy Emphasis On Playing One Pitch At A Time

The University of North Carolina, Wilmington has emerged as one of the most successful mid-major programs in college baseball. The Seahawks have an extensive approach to mental conditioning and a unique system for playing and practicing one pitch at a time.

WORKING ON THE MENTAL GAME IMPORTANT

"We have had a lot of physically-gifted players who work extremely hard and we really try to explore as much of the mental game as possible." Former pitching coach Scott Jackson (now at The University of North Carolina, Chapel Hill) said. "We had Brian Cain come in for a three day seminar in the fall and teach our coaches and players a system for working on the mental game, which has made a big difference for both players and coaches."

PITCHERS TAKE MENTAL GAME APPROACH TO BULLPEN

Jackson, one of the top young coaches in the country, found that he was spending the majority of his time in the bullpen working on mechanics work and did not invest enough time into the pitchers throwing competitive, game-like pens.

"I fell into the trap of always working on mechanics and

would rarely let the guys get after it from a competitive standpoint in the pen," Jackson said. "Now I have them throwing to a stand-in hitter every pitch, working with them to establish a consistent routine and focusing on their breath in-between each pitch, and really focusing on making quality pitches."

"The guys have responded positively, because they are simulating what they will be doing in a game: competing. I will admit it. I spent too much time preaching mechanics and not enough time getting the competitor to come out from inside our pitchers."

"I think I am like most coaches in that I would rather have a guy on the game mound with a bulldog mentality and less than great mechanics, than a guy with great mechanics and a less than aggressive mentality and I was coaching the opposite way. I was investing more time into mechanics than I was mentality."

HITTERS FOCUS ON QUALITY NOT QUANTITY

UNCW hitting coach Randy Hood, expressed how the Mental Game has helped his hitters to become more in control at the plate, give away fewer at-bats and focus on quality game-like reps, not just putting in their time in the cage.

"When I first started coaching, I felt that you would be successful largely to the degree of time and extra effort you put into hitting in the cages and getting a lot of reps," Hood said. "However, I have changed my perspective on that approach. I think that getting good quality swings with a game-like focus and a game-like process of going through your routine each and every swing, just like you are going to do in a game, is far more productive."

GAME-LIKE PRACTICE KEY

"We want our hitters to play one pitch at a time during games, but how often do we let them do that in practice?" asks Hood. "Practice makes permanent and it is unfair for me to ask any of our players to do anything in a game setting that they have not yet been able to do a hundred times in practice. If we want to play one pitch at a time in games, we need to get them playing one pitch at a time in practice. Nothing should change with their focus and mental game whether it is a practice or a game."

"There is a time when we will work on just swing mechanics during practice, but to put it all together in the game, the mental game can't be ignored. I would rather have a guy at the plate with a consistent mental process and an average swing than I would have a guy who has a picture perfect swing but an inconsistent, unreliable mindset."

SIGNAL LIGHT AWARENESS FOR HITTERS

Playing the game one pitch at a time is about having an awareness of where you are at physically, mentally and emotionally between each pitch. When you can stay in control of yourself, you give yourself the best chance for success by having quality at-bats and cutting down the number of at-bats you give away.

"Each of our hitters has a signal light sticker on their bat," Hood said. "They each have a red, yellow and green sticker that they use as a focal point on their bat between each pitch. We spent a lot of time talking with them about developing an awareness of their internal traffic light and when they start to struggle and what they can do to turn the at-bat around."

"We have them focus on the green label on the bat and take a good deep breath from their belly. If they can get a deep breath while focusing on the green dot, then the hitter knows they are in control of themselves and are playing one pitch at a time. As a coach, I can also see where my players are at mentally by being able to observe them going through their routine. I know if a player does something different than what is in their routine, they are either holding onto a previous pitch, or are in fast forward mode. Knowing my players routines allows me to remind players to check in and release before they give that at-bat away."

FOCAL POINTS – REMINDERS OF SUCCESS

All players at UNCW utilize a focal point in the outfield that they can turn to when the game starts speeding up on them, or if they realize that they are in a yellow or red light. That focal point serves as a box of positive thoughts that players can turn to for reassurance that they are in control and playing one pitch at a time.

"We use the focal point every day in the bullpen and on the mound," Jackson said. "I have written down what each pitchers focal point is so I know when they use it to help release. In the bullpen, I will often have the pitcher verbalize out loud what they are saying to themselves to get back in control. It is great for me to hear the self-talk they use to get back in-control because I can then build off of that and tailor my approach to each individual pitcher."

"I like seeing our hitters go to the focal point both on offense and defense," Hood said. "If we have a guy who makes an error, I want to see him turn his back to home plate, look at his focal point, pull his chest up and flush away the mistake. It is great for me because, as a coach, I can see a guy who makes an error, or misses a great pitch, go to their focal point, take a couple good breaths, release the negative and then get right back to playing one pitch at a time."

TURN A NEGATIVE INTO A POSITIVE

When a coach knows a players routines and releases, it's easier to notice them doing something good after a mistake or an error and praise them for handling the adversity the right way, quickly turning a negative into a positive.

"Being able to see them release and knowing what their focal points are allows us, as a coaching staff, to take a negative experience for a player, i.e. throwing a bad pitch, making an error, etc…, and it allows us to catch them being good," Jackson said. "In my coaching career I have always been looking for a way to turn a negative into a positive and if you can catch a player doing something good after they make a mistake, if you can catch them going to their focal point and flushing the negative, you can then praise that player for doing everything they can do to get back to the present moment and playing pitch by pitch."

NEW TOILET INSTALLED IN THE DUGOUT

UNCW recently built a new clubhouse and constructed major renovations to their facilities. The most important addition to their program might be the new plastic "Flush

It" toilet in the home team's dugout.

"We have a small toilet bank that our players and staff will flush when they make a mistake or things are not going their way," Hood said. "Every time one of our guys flushes the toilet you have to laugh and that helps lighten the mood."

"Baseball is a tough game that can beat you up because no matter what you do, you are always going to fail more than you succeed. When our guys flush the toilet and laugh, it loosens them up and allows their true talents to come out."

"Our guys are ultra-competitive and have dedicated their lives to playing baseball. That being the case, they tend to all try too hard and put too much pressure on themselves to be perfect. The toilet serves as a reminder that this game is fun and that you can't take thing too seriously or your performance is going to suffer. Our guys will often come into the dugout after making an error or striking out and flush the toilet; you can almost instantly see the weight come off of their shoulders."

PITCHERS DON'T GET HITTERS OUT, HITTERS DO

The process of how you go about your business in the long term is more important than the results that you in the short term. Most players fall into the trap of results thinking and forget that baseball is a game where the process is what you must focus on to give yourself the best chance for success long term.

"I used to be a big results guy," Jackson said. "But in baseball you can't always control the results. All that you can control is yourself and your APE: Attitude/Appearance (Body

Language), Process/Perspective and Effort. If you can take care of yourself and your APE, you are doing everything in your power to be successful."

"You see pitchers all the time who throw great pitches, but give up hits. Likewise you see pitchers who get lucky and throw lousy pitches and get outs. Baseball is unfair like that. It takes a mentally tough pitcher to understand that the only thing they can do is throw the ball where they want to, after that, it is out of their hands. Pitchers DO NOT get hitters out, they make pitches. Hitters get themselves out. The more good pitches you throw, the more hitters get themselves out. There is a correlation between the two."

DH STAND IN HITTER A FIXTURE IN BULLPEN

Steve Zawrotny, the director of www.baseballfit.com, has developed a great tool for the bullpen called the Designated Hitter. The DH is a six foot tall replica of a batter that lives in the UNCW bullpen and takes a beating, but never complains.

"The DH has been great for our pitchers," Jackson said. "Most pitchers don't like having a hitter on their own team, or a pitcher who stands in because they do not want to hit a teammate when working on throwing the ball inside. Subsequently when we practice going inside, our pitchers get timid. That can't happen if you want to be successful."

"Some guys think that throwing to the inside of the plate without a hitter in there is the same thing as having a hitter in there. Not true. The task changes visually for the pitcher and that often results in a different mindset, a tentative mindset, when attacking the inside part of home plate."

"The DH looks just like a real hitter and we use it in all of our bullpens. We stress to our pitchers that every pitch in the bullpen should be with a game-like mentality. As their pitching coach, if I don't have a stand-in hitter, I am limiting their ability to make the bullpen game-like, because they will never make a pitch in a game without a hitter in the batter's box."

"Our pitchers have really enjoyed throwing to the DH. They can come inside with an aggressive pitch thought and blow it up. If they hit the DH, nobody cares. That is the type of aggressiveness that I work very hard at developing in our pitchers. Every bullpen in America should have a stand in hitter."

KEY POINTS FOR REVIEW:

- **Working on the mental game in practice is important.**

- **Focus on quality of work over the quantity of work.**

- **Every player should have a focal point that they can use as a reminder of their hard work and why they should be successful.**

- **As a coach and teammate, catching players who are doing things the right way after a mistake and praising them for their positive reactions is important for team success.**

- **Developing awareness of your internal traffic light and knowing when you are in a green light or a red light mentality is critical for consistent performance.**

Chapter 15 | SERRANO SHARES SUCCESS SECRETS OF PITCHING

Top College Coach Shares Mental Toughness Training Tips For Pitchers

Dave Serrano is no stranger to pitching success. He is currently the Head Baseball Coach at The University of Tennessee (2012-pesent) and former head coach at Cal State Fullerton (2007-2011) and the University of California, Irvine (2005-2007). He was the pitching coach at The University of Tennessee (1995-1996) and at Cal State Fullerton (1997-2004) and guided the Titans pitching staff to the 2004 NCAA National Championship.

Serrano has coached some of the games top pitchers having tutored one of Major League Baseball All-Stars Chad Cordero (2005) and Ricky Romero (2011), and 2004 NCAA College World Series MVP Jason Windsor. Serrano was willing to share some of his pitching insight as to what he feels makes a mentally tough pitcher.

MOVING FROM MECHANICS INTO MENTAL GAME

A coach who spent the majority of his time working on pitchers with their mechanics and conditioning, Serrano says that he has come a long way in what he believes makes a good pitcher.

"As a pitching coach I have come to realize that it is not about natural ability, it isn't about physical size and strength; it is more about the mentality that leads pitchers to success." Serrano said. "Being consistent and reaching their capabilities as a pitcher, day in and day out, is more of a mindset and an attitude than it is a physical skill. I did not always believe that, but as I get more experience and am around this game longer, I am finding out it is largely about a pitcher's mentality."

SELF-CONTROL AND COMFORT IN THE SYSTEM

In his book *Heads Up Baseball,* Dr. Ken Ravizza writes about how you must be in control of yourself before you can control your performance and how you have very little control of what goes on around you, but total control of how you choose to respond to it. For many pitchers who make the jump from high school to college or from college to the professional ranks, it is often the challenge of learning a new system, or dealing with the more intense and challenging game and practice environments that cause pitchers to fall short of their potential.

"As a pitcher you have got to be in control of yourself and be comfortable in the system in which you trying to pitch." Says Serrano, "That is why game-like practice is so important. If you are not practicing under game-like simulated stressful conditions as there will be in a game, I think that once you put a pitcher in that competitive situation, there is a tendency for paralysis by analysis and the pitcher is not able to compete like they are capable of, because they have too much information that they are trying to mentally process. They can't keep the game simple and let their true talent come out."

GAME-LIKE PRACTICE IS KEY

Making game-like practice is something that coaches often struggle with. Scripting bullpens, or having two pitchers throw simulated innings in which they compete against each other for the number of quality pitches puts the pitcher in a competitive environment as opposed to just "throwing" their bullpen practice with no stand in hitter or person charting pitches. Creating competition in practice simulates game-like conditions and establishes a familiarity among players with the competitive atmosphere of the real games.

"As much as we try to simulate game situations in practice, if the young man who is throwing the ball is not going through the simulation with a mental game-like competitiveness, it is going to be tough for him to succeed once he actually gets put in that situation." Serrano says, "One of the things that I used to do was to try and get my pitchers to pretend that their bullpen was actually them throwing in front of 25,000 people in Omaha. I have recently taken a new approach and now I try to get my pitchers to prepare as if they were throwing in what will be their next outing."

"Instead of having them prepare in their bullpens like they are throwing in a regional or Omaha, I want them to prepare like they are throwing in the first live scrimmage of the year or whatever their next outing will be. We always try to simulate the pitchers next outing when throwing in the bullpen. We will progress in that manner over the course of the season till we get to the point where we can talk about Regionals and Omaha. I have found that the pitchers can put themselves in a competitive mindset during their bullpens that more closely resembles their next outing. It ties in better with our philosophy which is that we can prepare to have a good outing in our next outing, we are controlling everything that we can, and that is all we can really do."

BULLPEN IS A CRITICAL WORK ENVIRONMENT

In college, many times pitchers will find practice boring and unproductive because there is only a limited amount they can do. They do not hit, and typically will not spend as much time fielding as position players will. Bullpen sessions thus become of utmost importance and for the pitcher and pitching coach are a time where they can get together to do some quality work and improvement.

"As a pitcher, the bullpen atmosphere is your game," Serrano said. "The way you perspire, the way you breathe, your timing, everything needs to be of the quality that it would be if you were trying to win the biggest game of your career. We do this so that when we go into games, the pitchers can feel like they have been there before".

"Everything has to be the same as it would if you were in a game, if you are in the set position and you have self-doubts about the pitch you are throwing, you have got to step off. We practice stepping off in the bullpen just like we would in a game. We don't want to develop bad habits of balking in the bullpen, or throwing pitches that we are not fully committed to," says Serrano. "What we do in the bullpen is what we will do in the game. We will even go to the point of visualizing that a runner has a big lead, or visualizing that one of our infielders is out of position, so that we will step off and not be caught off guard if that happens in a game."

"If you do anything short of that, than you are really defeating the purpose of your bullpen. We see so many pitchers who come into college and just want to go to the bullpen and throw. There is no focus, no plan and the pitcher has no idea what they are working on. They are doing what I call aerobic pitching. That type of focus and mentality in the pen is only good for one thing: developing bad habits."

"You should be trying to execute every pitch to a stand in hitter like you would in a game." Says Serrano "We never let our pitchers throw to just a catcher. When will they ever have that look in a game?"

PITCHING COACH MUST BE PRESENT

Serrano also feels that it is critical that as the pitching coach, he be with his pitchers when they are throwing their bullpens.

"I am with them 99.9% of the time that they are in the bullpen. If I am going to help call their game from the dugout, then I need to know what they can do, what is working for them, and they need to know what I want them to do in the game. I will simulate counts and pitch sequences with them in the bullpen, just like I would in a game."

THE FOUNDATION FOR SUCCESS

Serrano has been a part of three of the most prominent college baseball programs in the country at UCI, Cal State Fullerton and now Tennessee. Having worked with great coaches such as George Horton, Rick Vanderhook and Rod Delmonico, he feels that one of the experiences that separates the good from the great programs is their belief and philosophy around the mental aspects of the game.

"In all the programs that I have been a part of, the mental game has been a huge part of our success. I think as coaches we were able to develop a language that allowed us to communicate the mental part of the game much more effectively with our players," says Serrano. "I think that in order for a coach to get his players to buy into the mental game, the coaching staff has to buy into it first. Your players are going to buy into whatever you believe in. If a coach is not 100% behind the belief that the mental game is important, than the players are going to read that and not buy into it either."

MISCONCEPTIONS OF THE MENTAL GAME

Many coaches are turned off by the mental game because they feel that it slows the game down or that it takes their players out of a natural rhythm and gets them thinking too much. The reality, however, due to the slow nature of the game and large amount of failure built into it, players already have a tendency to overthink the game.

The mental game can be practice just like fielding a ground ball or hitting. Motor learning research shows that anytime you try to learn a new skill, be it physical or mental in nature, there is a learning curve that takes place and you will have to think about the skill before it becomes automatic. Many coaches don't take time to work through the initial over analysis stages of the mental game, where a player's performance may decline due to an increased amount of cognitive thought process before an increase in performance once the athlete is more comfortable with their new approach to the game.

Subsequently, coaches often leave their athletes high and dry when the going gets tough and the pressure is on, because the athlete has not practiced and developed the skills of self-control and self-regulation needed to succeed in pressure packed situations.

"You don't want your athletes out there thinking the mental game," says Serrano. "The mental game needs to become part of their routine and part of their mechanics. If you are out there thinking physical mechanics, or thinking mental game, you are not performing. The mental game does not slow the game down in terms of tempo, but it does slow it down in terms of a focus on results and the athlete's internal pressure. The mental game allows you to be in control of yourself when you need to perform in the most pressure packed situation, and on those days when you don't feel well, or don't have you're best stuff physically. The mental game is a system that allows athletes to play well when they don't feel well."

"A big part of my philosophy in coaching is that we will control what we can control, and in the game of baseball there is only so much that you can control. What you can control is a minimal part of the game and that is why the mental game is so important, because you can't control all that much in baseball. It becomes critical that you control what you can, so that you are giving yourself the best chance for success. As a pitcher, once that ball leaves your hand, there is nothing that you can do to control what is going to happen, so you must be in control of yourself before you throw the pitch to give yourself the best chance that you will achieve the desired result of putting the ball where you want to put it."

FAILURE IS AN UNAVOIDABLE PART OF THE GAME

Serrano also recognizes the great amount of failure built into baseball as a reason why the mental game is so important.

"The best hitters in the game get out 70% of the time. That is very mentally draining for them. If you can tell me someone in any other profession that can have a successful career failing 7 out of 10 times, I'd be impressed. A doctor or a teacher that fails 70% of the time won't have a job." Serrano said. "So for a pitcher who can throw a great pitch and give up a hit, and throw a lousy pitch and get an out, it just goes to show that the mental game and evaluating yourself by the process and the things that you can control is critical. Unfortunately, many players still evaluate their success on outcome and factors outside of their control."

CONNECTIONS FROM THE FIELD TO LIFE

Serrano tries to teach his players how to make connections between what happens on the field to what happens in everyday life. He feels that coaches need to do more than just teach the skills of the game, they also should teach how skills and experiences on the diamond apply to life outside of baseball.

"Baseball is so unique in that there is no time clock, you have to play 9 innings and you have to record 27 outs, and it is the team that is most prepared and plays the best that day that is going to be successful," says Serrano. "I think that the Cal State Fullerton National Championship team in 2004 was not the most talented team in the country, but we were the most mentally prepared team that year. The mental preparation that goes into getting ready for a practice, a game or a season is the same type of preparation that these athletes will have to do when they are done playing and are out working in the real world. In the real world, like in baseball, success often finds the ones who have prepared the most."

POSITIVE BODY LANGUAGE CRITICAL PART OF SUCCESS

Serrano recognizes the importance of positive body language as one of the skills that he teachers to his pitchers.

"A lot of times I can tell how a pitchers bullpen is going without even seeing the results of their pitches," says Serrano. "I can tell by their body language, tempo and mannerisms whether or not they are throwing well. One of the things we work on is trying to get them to be consistent from a body language and mannerism perspective, whether they are throwing great or lousy. We are in control of how we respond to everything that is happening and if we wear our emotions on our sleeves, we are giving a lot of information to the other team that they can then use against us."

"We like to use the buzz words 'Fake it till you make it' and 'Act different than how you feel'. If a pitcher can fake their body language into acting like they are throwing great when they don't have great stuff, they will be that much closer to regaining their good stuff. The other option is to carry yourself like to feel, and on the days you don't feel well, let the coach and the rest of the pitching staff know that you are going to get hit hard and they should be ready to take you out. That is a weak mindset and one that unfortunately we still see a lot from pitchers. Confidence and composure are skills just like a good pick-off move, and they need to be worked on daily."

MENTAL GAME PAYS BIG DIVIDENDS IN TITLE RUN

Serrano sites Jason Windsor and Scott Sarver as two of the pitchers he has had the pleasure of working with that developed their mental game and how their work paid off and was a large reason why the Titans were able to win the National Championship in 2004.

"In 2003, I remember taking a trip to the mound in Fullerton's first game vs. LSU in The College World Series to see Jason Windsor," recalls Serrano. "He was a pitcher who had come out of nowhere that year to be one of the best pitchers in the country. Going into game one in Omaha, we felt that he was as prepared as anyone could be. Jason is a true strike thrower and a true competitor who had proved it over an entire course of the season playing against the top teams in the country. I remember going out to the mound and he told me that he was having a tough time breathing. That just proved to me that no matter how good you are, even if you are a stud like Jason Windsor, the game can still speed up on you, and if you don't have a practiced pre-pitch routine, and something to go to when the game is in fast forward, you will never be able to be a big game pitcher. Jason was able to regain control of himself and would go on to win that game in 2003. What he did in 2004 in Omaha, however, was just amazing. If it were not for his diligence in developing his mental game, I don't think he would have had the success that he did. I think that the experience and the awareness that he got in 2003 prepared him to pitch at the level of excellence that earned him the College World Series MVP in 2004."

"I tip my cap to a guy like Scott Sarver," recalls Serrano. "Here's a player who in 2004 was not getting a lot of innings and could have very easily packed it in and felt that he was a part of a special team, but didn't really contribute, but that he'll just be along for the ride. Scott did nothing of the sort. He prepared himself on a daily basis with his bullpens and dry mechanics as if he was going to pitch that weekend for us. He took the mental approach like he was going to be a starting pitcher on the weekend. He was mentally prepared to pitch and he did not get a lot of innings for us during the regular season. We called his number in the regional, and he went out and did what he had been doing all year in his preparation. He then went out and did the same thing in Omaha. That takes a lot of mental toughness to stay with it when you are not getting the innings or playing time that you want during the season. If he had not taken so much diligence in his preparation, I don't think that the game would have rewarded him like it did."

MENTAL GAME IMPORTANT FOR SUCCESS IN OMAHA

Serrano also talked about one of the "Mental Game Tools" that he and the pitching staff used that season and in Omaha.

"One of the things we did in 2004 was bring a water bottle full of dirt from the bullpen at Goodwin Field, our home field in Fullerton, and sprinkle some of that dirt on the mounds at Rosenblatt Stadium in Omaha. We did that because we wanted our pitchers to feel that the mound in Rosenblatt was our mound. That we owned that mound, it was our dirt, and that the mound was built for us. It was a simple yet very powerful way to help our pitchers mentally become more comfortable with what can very often be a very uncomfortable atmosphere."

ADVICE FOR PLAYING AT THE NEXT LEVEL

Serrano also offered a few tips of advice for players who want to play at the next level.

"I think players have to be open to learning a new system and be open to suggestions from coaches on helping them to become better," says Serrano. "The players that feel they have all the answers will come in and fall short. The athletes that buy into the system will work harder and, subsequently, have more success."

LEARNING FROM MISTAKES IS KEY FOR GROWTH

He also shared how he learned over the years that people are people and that pitchers are pitchers. He shared that one of the things that has helped him become a successful pitching coach is learning from his mistakes.

"As coaches we can over coach young men. And be a roadblock in their careers. Wes Littleton came to us at Cal State Fullerton as one of the top high school pitchers in Southern California. As a freshman I thought there were some things that he absolutely had to change in his mechanics to be consistently successful at our level. Well, I did Wes a disservice that first year as I think he fell into the paralysis by analysis mode and did not perform like he was capable of because I over coached him and tried to get him to change some things. The following year I told him that I was going to take a different approach and try to work with him more on being consistent mentally and within his own physical pitching style. He had a tremendous sophomore season, was an All-American, made Team USA and has since gone on to have a successful professional career. That experience reassured me that as coaches we need to often put our egos away and make sure that we coach our athletes as unique individuals, not coaching the athlete to be a robot."

"I don't believe that mechanics are the same for everyone. I try not to coach style out of pitchers. I try to coach to their style. I think you have to try to coach each pitcher differently and you cannot try to mold them to be exactly alike."

FAVORITE MEMORIES OF THE MENTAL GAME

Serrano also shared one of his favorite mental game experiences that happened during the Titans improbable National Championship run in 2004.

"The night before we were playing Texas in the Championship Series, and would be facing their ace and crafty lefthander J.P. Howell, we had all the players meet in a conference room in the hotel" recalls Serrano. "As we are talking to the team about the next day's schedule and getting ready to watch some video tape of J.P. Howell, in comes our pitcher Scott Sarver, all decked out in Texas Longhorn gear to the surprise of all our position players who at that point wanted to rip all the cloths off of him and beat him down."

"As we were watching the video of Howell pitch, Sarver was going through the same mechanics and mannerisms that we were seeing on TV and our hitters were standing up, imaging themselves hitting against Scott, acting as Howell. In that "visual inning" we scored three runs and, ironically enough, the next day in Game One of the Championship Series against Texas and J.P. Howell, we scored three runs in the first inning.

Most people don't know that we actually scored three runs off him in the first inning the night before in the conference room at the hotel. Mental imagery doesn't always work that way, but if you are not doing mental imagery, I think you are leaving a lot of your preparation and game time confidence to chance."

"Our big motto in 2004 was 'Get To The Next Pitch', and that reemphasized the fact that you can't control what has just happened, you can only control how you choose to respond to it. We had lost a tough game against South Carolina, and when we got back to the hotel, we made our guys put their jerseys back on and when they were ready, they took them off and threw then into a pile as a way to release the loss. Throwing the jersey down was symbolic of throwing away the loss and you could really see the weight come off of the guys, especially the ones who were in that same situation the previous year when we had lost the two games to Stanford after having started out the World Series 2-0."

HAVING A MENTOR KEY TO COACHES DEVELOPMENT

Serrano sites Dr. Ken Ravizza as one of the people that has taught him a lot about the mental game of baseball. When asked if he could give one message to the readers about the importance of the mental game, he replied:

"If I had to give one message to the readers about the mental game, I would say believe in it, trust in it and understand that it is all about the process. When you take the results out of it you can focus on what you can control and you when you focus on what you can control, you are giving yourself the best chance to get your desired result. We all want the results, but we need to know how to handle the bad results. Learning how to handle the bad results is a huge step in learning how to consistently get to the good results. The mental game is a big factor in the success of players and coaches. The mental game should be taken very seriously and you should take the time to learn and teach it."

KEY POINTS FOR REVIEW:

- It is critical that pitching coaches work with pitchers on both The Mental Game and mechanics.

- Self-control and comfort in the team pitching system is key for pitchers to have success.

- Game-like practice is key for pitchers becoming more comfortable in pressure situations.

- Bullpen work is the most important part of the pitchers practice and should be treated seriously with the pitching coach present.

- Success breeds success, and spending time around winning programs will teach you what it takes to be successful.

- It is an unfortunate misconception in athletics that routines and The Mental Game will slow down your tempo and make you think too much.

- Failure is an inevitable part sport that every athlete must embrace and learn from.

- It is important for coaches to help players make connection from the game of baseball to life.

- Positive body language and a positive attitude are important parts of giving yourself the best chance for success.

- The Mental Game pays big dividends in big games.

Chapter 16 | WOLFORTH DISCUSSES MENTAL TOUGHNESS TIPS FOR PITCHING

Mental Game of Pitching Can Be Developed With System and Structure

Ron Wolforth, director of Pitching Central, a Houston Texas based pitching development facility has developed a total pitching development program called "The Athletic Pitcher." Wolforth shared how he teaches the mental aspects of pitching performance and works with pitchers at his pitching boot camp to produce more mentally tough and competitive pitchers.

PERSONAL EXPERIENCE PAVES THE WAY

Wolforth was slightly below average college pitcher who stood about 5'9", and threw in the range of 86-89 MPH. The driving force behind what he does today in his work with pitchers was motivated by his own personal experience that left him wondering how someone who threw pretty hard, had great attitude and work ethic, did not have more success than he did in college?

"I would always hear coaches and players in TV interviews after games say 'We won because we wanted it.' Hearing this frustrated me because no one wanted it more than I did in college. So I started to ask myself, why was I an underachiever? Through my experience I realized that work ethic and intelligence are important factors in pitching success, but not the sole ingredient in determining who will be a successful pitcher. So I started to research and critically analyze why my performance was not as good as it could have been, and why so many pitchers fall short of their potential."

LACK OF TALENT IS AN EXCUSE

When pitchers fall short of success, it is often said that they just didn't have enough talent. Wolforth believes that using a lack of talent is often a coach's excuse for a lack of coaching ability.

"Coaches will often say that a 'lack of talent' is why pitchers fall short of their full capability. I can agree with that to a degree, but to me that is a cop-out response. I am not satisfied with the 'lack of talent' answer because there is just not enough substance behind it."

THE CHALLENGE IS GETTING OUT OF YOUR OWN WAY

Many times when you have a pitcher or a player that wants to be very successful, works extremely hard and is intelligent, the biggest obstacle for these athletes is often getting out of their own way.

"I truly believe that there are two things that can make a tremendous difference for a pitcher, and that is developing awareness and perspective. If you have awareness and perspective you can then start to develop what a lot of coaches would call "mental toughness" or "mental tenacity". What I mean by awareness is, 'knowing what exactly is happening at that moment'. What I did for the most part in college, and a lot of players will do this, is try to please the coaches in what they expected me to do, rather than having an awareness of what was happening on the mound.

Awareness is the recognition whether I'm throwing it high or low or why I'm getting behind early in the count? Awareness is identifying why I'm struggling to put hitters away and what is the reason I am not being as successful as I can be. Constant awareness of what is happening at the present moment is critical because it allows you to make necessary the adjustments to perform at a level of excellence."

COACHES CAN'T ASSUME

One of the issues that Wolforth had to overcome, as many pitchers do, is that often his coaches expected that he knew what was happening, that he knew why he could not locate his pitches and that he knew what he needed to work on to get better. Many times, athletes do not know what it is they need to work on to improve and are subsequently written off as mental midgets or someone that 'just doesn't have it'. As coaches we need to constantly be communicating with our pitchers about what they need to do to be successful and what they need to do to improve.

"I hear the traditional pitching coach platitudes of 'get ahead, just throw strikes, relax', all the time, but they are very empty in terms of direction. They are not much help to a pitcher. It would be like me telling you that the secret of the stock market is to buy low and sell high, or that the secret to a good marriage is communication. It is true, but very empty. What athletes need is specifics on how to do it."

"I had a coach come to me once at the mound and say 'Ron, your falling behind hitters, your leaving the ball up, and you are not getting your curveball over for strikes, and this will be your last hitter if you can't do it.' What he said was just about as helpful as a drunken guy in the stands yelling 'Hey Wolforth, you got to throw strikes'. I said to myself, I knew that already. What I needed, and not necessarily at that time during the game, but more so during the previous practices and preparation up to the game was how I could have made those in-game adjustments, based off of my awareness and the feedback that I was getting from the game."

COACHES NEED TO KNOW PITCHERS AS PEOPLE

Coaches are often quick on giving mechanical advice or to label a pitcher, but rarely give the pitcher the skills necessary to develop the necessary awareness or the ability to deal with pressure packed situations. One of the things that Wolforth recommends for coaches is to first spend the time to get a better understanding of who their pitchers are as people and what their pitching instructional background has been before jumping to critiquing their pitching style.

"I think that the first thing coaches need to learn to do, and it comes right from Stephen Covey's "Seven Habits Of Highly Effective People" is "Seek first to understand, then to be understood." So often pitching coaches want to make a quick fix on a guy with mechanics, but they need to do a better job drawing out the information from the pitcher about what they feel and are experiencing while they are pitching. A pitcher might be leaving the ball up because they are rushing, so we make a mechanical fix to keep them back, but the reason the ball is up is because the pitcher is mentally in fast forward mode. They are putting too much pressure on themselves and trying to do too much. Too often we use labels that a kid is easily rattled or gets frustrated easily, or is a chocker, but have we taught them how to respond correctly and to be in-control of themselves in those situations?"

"Often when a pitcher makes a move to a higher level, high school to college or college to pro, the new pitching coach will recommend mechanical adjustments the first day of practice. What they should do instead is observe the pitchers strengths and weaknesses and work with them to improve their own pitching style. Attempting to understand a pitcher means that you have to honor that pitcher's past, and you have to understand what they have done and who they have worked with. That doesn't mean that you can't make changes, but we have to know where a pitcher is coming from and what they have been taught in the past."

COACHES CAN NOT COOKIE CUT PITCHERS

We as coaches often fall into the rut of trying to teach all our pitchers the same way mechanically. We teach them what we feel to be the best mechanical approach. Wolforth feels that this cookie cutter approach can often hurt more than help pitchers.

"If I told Andy Pettit that he needed to look more like Roger Clemens at the foot strike position on video because Roger has 7 Cy-Young awards, that would not work for Andy. If you watch a big league game, many pitchers do not throw the same. Pitchers have their own individual style. We as coaches have to do a better job working with them in their style."

PITCHING FROM THE INSIDE OUT

Pitchers often need more work on their pre-pitch routine and ability to stay emotionally in control of themselves than they do on mechanical work to help them stay mechanically consistent. Wolforth explains how he teaches his pitchers to pitch from inside out, not from the outside in.

"Pitchers need routines because if they don't have routines, they are at risk of having the circumstances around them dictate how they respond, rather than controlling themselves within the context of the surrounding environment. You have to pitch from the inside out because the outside is full of circumstances outside of your control. The chances of things going not well in a game are 100%. If you are thinking about being perfect, that is rarely going to happen. What you need to do is have a routine that allows you to stay within yourself and allows you to stay on track. A routine that allows the chaos going on around you to be just that, around you, not inside of you... We need to focus on the things that we can control and let go of the things that we cannot. That is far easier said than done, believe me."

GAME-LIKE PRACTICE IS IMPORTANT

Game-like practice is critical to preparing pitchers for the ever-changing game environment and Wolforth offers some interesting drills on how to make your bullpens more game like.

"Typically baseball practices are very routine, predictable and stale, while games are the complete opposite. Pitchers often develop practice habits or routines that allow them to get comfortable. Then when they get into a game, they develop anxiety because it is so different from the consistent and predictable practice environment that they are used to. The pitcher needs to learn that if they can stick to their inner routine, they will be able to handle all the other stuff that is going on around them. At our facility in Houston, we will have pitchers go through their routines as we try to create havoc for them so that they don't know what is coming. This makes their practice more game-like."

MAKING ADJUSTMENTS = MENTAL TOUGHNESS

Wolforth feels that a mentally tough pitcher is someone who can make the necessary adjustments during a game from pitch to pitch.

"We believe that the determining factor in whether a pitcher will be successful or unsuccessful is simply in his ability to adjust. What does adjustment mean? It means that you have to be emotionally and mentally stable enough to recognize what just happened and then what your adjustments need to be. You also have to be in the present moment. You can't be in the past or the future. You have to be in the moment. You also have to practice adjusting. The environment, whether it be the weather, the umpire, the strike zone, or the field conditions, can change from pitch to pitch and you have to be able to make those subtle adjustments to keep yourself on track. It is like driving down the road and recognizing that you are drifting into the other lane. The bad drivers jerk the wheel to get the car back where it needs to be. Good drivers are always looking down the road and making small, constant minor adjustments to keep them on track. There are a whole bunch of people with great stuff in this game that will never make it because they are unable to make adjustments on the fly in game time from pitch to pitch, and that is a skill that needs to be developed like a good pick play or a curveball."

MENTAL & PHYSICAL GAME ARE INTERWOVEN

Wolforth also stressed that the mental game and the physical game are interwoven and should be viewed as one and the same, not two separate types of practice.

"I am a big fan of Ken Ravizza and have followed his stuff for a long time, and we believe that the mental game cannot be separate from the physical game. You have to be working on it all the time. If you ask any of our pitchers they will tell you that the mental game is interwoven into what we do, and that any time they throw a baseball they are always working on their mental game.

COMPETITIVE DRILLS KEY PART OF PRACTICE

Wolforth shared some of the drills that he uses at the academy which specifically address the mental toughness development of his pitchers.

"We will do competitive bullpens in which you compete with the guy next to you—kind of like dueling bullpens. We will do a series of fastball, curveball, changeups, where the fastball has to be to the extension side, then the breaking ball has to be in for a strike, then the changeup has to be in for a strike. We will have team A and team B compete against each other with some extra conditioning on the line. We play that the first team to ten points wins. The first guy from each team will throw a fastball, if it is a quality pitch, the next guy on our team will throw the curveball. If that is a quality pitch, the next guy will throw the changeup. If that is a quality pitch the next guy will throw the fastball again. If someone missed the pitch the next guy gets to throw it. It is very much like the basketball game HORSE but for pitchers. The nice thing is that the pitcher never knows what pitch they will be throwing until they toe the rubber because the previous pitchers pitch dictates what the next guy throws. It is very game-like."

"The competitiveness of the game builds in the game-like pressure and the pitcher also has the time to process their pitch in between pitches and think about what has just happened. They don't have much time to get frustrated with a bad pitch and we view frustration as a focus on the problem. The focus needs to be on the solution, not the problem. Once they start thinking of the solution, the problem goes away. They don't have time to focus on the problem. Much like in a game, they have to make minor adjustments and then get back on the bump and deliver."

"We also let the guys talk trash to each other to try and simulate what they might get in a game from the other team or from hostile fans. Some nights we don't let them make any sounds or talk at all. We can also have the catchers squeeze them to death to simulate the tight umpire and that gives us a chance to really see how the pitcher will respond to a tight ump in a game. We can then coach them on how they should respond. There is a lot of variation with this drill we can go through 6 pitchers bullpens in about the time it takes to do two or three, and it is much more focused and competitive. We will also chart and track how long it takes them to get to their ten points and we can evaluate them that way as well, so that the pitcher walks away from the bullpen with solid, objective information. You might have lost the game, but you went from taking 25 pitches to get your 10 points, to only needing 14 pitches. That also reemphasizes the process over the outcome because in this game, you can only control what you do. We call that the process."

"One of the nice things that happens is when our pitchers start to lose control and blow up during some of these competitive drills, our older and more mature pitchers will go over, put there arm around the guy and tell him 'hey, here is what is happening'. When they hear it from a peer it is much more meaningful than when it comes from a coach, and I think that happens in great college and high school programs."

"We are also big on gathering objective information. We feel that you can't improve unless you know where you currently are and have something to compare your performances against. The pitcher can see with the radar gun or with charting that there is accountability to what we do, and we feel that they respond much better to objective data than subjective data, or us telling them, 'Hey, that was a good pen today'. They want us to prove it to them with the numbers and the facts."

PROCESS OVER OUTCOME APPROACH IMPORTANT

Wolforth emphasizes the process over the outcome with his pitchers. He stresses that because the pitcher has complete control of the process he should spend the majority of his time focusing on what he can control. He also indicated that like a good physical skill, the mental game takes a while to develop and is something that we are always working on.

"The mental game is just like going into the weight room and doing the bench press. You wouldn't go into the weight room, bench for 15 hours and expect to walk out being a lot stronger and feeling confident that you have a great bench press. The mental game is a process. You might be weak at first like you would in a bench press, but if you can work the process and stick with it over time, you will build a foundation and get stronger, just like you would if you lifted consistently over a longer period of time."

"A lot of times the mental toughness gets to be a story in and of itself. People will start to think of mental toughness as something that you have or you don't, and I don't think that is true. I think that mental toughness is something that is constantly evolving in the face of adversity. It is something that you need to build over time and through experiencing challenges. For example, Roger Clemens and my 8 year old son can both improve their mental game today. Too often we label people as being mentally weak. I think we all have a mental game and some of us are simply further down the path of developing those skills than others."

"The beauty of the mental game is that there is no end. I don't view it as a 'Here is your diploma, you have now graduated from the mental game' type of deal. The mental game is something that you are always working on and some days you have better days than others, just like with physical skills. I find that those pitchers and coaches who think they are at the top of their class will probably find out that they are in the wrong class. The mental game is a lifelong process and mental skills are life skills that athletes will use well beyond their baseball careers."

KEY POINTS FOR REVIEW:

- Lack of talent in an athlete is often an excuse as to why they fall short of their potential. There must be more substance to the reason why we fall short of our potential.

- As an athlete, the challenge is getting out of your own way and not beating yourself, but making the opponent beat you.

- Coaches can't assume that their players know everything Talk and get to know your players as people and find out where they are coming from and what their previous experience has been.

- Coaches cannot cookie cut a pitcher's mechanics. They must work with them to create a style that works for the individual.

- Pitching from the inside out is about finding out who you are and having an awareness as to what you need to do to be at your best.

- Game-like practice is important part of developing mental toughness, and competitive drills are a key part of making you comfortable with being uncomfortable.

- Making adjustments is representative of mental toughness.

- The mental and physical game is interwoven. You cannot work on one without the other and we cannot separate mental game work from physical game work.

- Coaches need to emphasize a process over outcome approach.

PART 3

More Mental Game Systems and Strategies You Can Use

Visit www.SoWhatNextPitch.com/EXTRAS For BONUS Mental Conditioning Material & FREE Peak Performance Training Tools

Chapter 17 | THE BEST AND WORST
OF SUMMER BASEBALL

Mental Conditioning Practice With The
Nation's Top Collegiate Baseball Players

Baseball is a unique sport: the defense has possession of the ball; self-preservation concerns can be high; and if a player strikes out or makes an error, everyone sees this failure. In fact, the rules of baseball are such that every error an athlete makes is counted and the very best players (i.e., those who end up in the Hall of Fame) are successful when they fail only seven out of ten times with the bat in their hands. Thus, it's critical for baseball players to base their standard of success on more than outcome and end results (e.g., batting average, number of pitching wins, etc...).

Before they make it to the Major Leagues, many of collegiate baseball's most talented and successful players compete over the summer in the highly competitive Cape Cod Baseball League. Because of the high level of competition on the Cape, the athletes' skills are tested every day and professional scouts hunt this League for future Major League Baseball stars.

The Cape Cod Baseball League, therefore, serves as a training ground for athletes to develop the mindset necessary to perform well and focus on their performance rather than the outcome and end results. This is important because *performance outcome in baseball is largely dependent on factors outside of one's control.* In baseball, an athlete can do everything right (successful process) and still fail (undesired outcome). This chapter describes several mental conditioning strategies I used to help Cape Cod League athletes with performance focus when I worked as an assistant coach in the league for the Cotuit Kettleers in 2001.

GOAL-SETTING

The athletes established personal goals in writing before the season. Those goal sheets were specific to the player's position, season on the Cape, and baseball career. Typical questions were: Why do you play baseball? What is your long-term goal for your baseball career, short-term goal for this summer? What are your three strengths you have as a pitcher or hitter? What can you do on a daily basis to help reach these goals?, etc...

Having the players' goals written down made it easier to communicate about what kind of knowledge the player had regarding goal-setting, outcome vs. process goals, expectations, and what type of mental conditioning the player had been exposed to at his school's program. Of the 25 goal sheets reviewed, the predominant answer was that their career goal was to get drafted, and that their short-term goal was to have a good summer on the Cape and get noticed by scouts.

Unfortunately, very few players had specific plans. Some players did identify that a good summer would mean hitting .300. (A total of five players from the 200+ players on the Cape hit .300 or better that summer.) Most goals were outcome goals concerning batting average or number of strikeouts—things based largely on factors outside the players' control.

Conversations with the athletes about their goals usually went something like this:

"What is your long-term goal?"

"My long term goal is to get drafted and be a successful pro ball player."

"To get drafted, what do you need to do?"

"Have a good summer here in the Cape, hit .300, and impress the scouts."

"To hit .300 what do you need to do?"

"I need to consistently hit the ball hard."

"To consistently hit the ball hard, what do you need to do?"

"I need to get the fat part of the bat on the ball."

"To get the fat part of the bat on the ball, what do you need to do?"

"I need to see the ball and take a good swing."

""To see the ball well and take a good swing, what do you need to do?"

This line of questioning outlines the importance of process goals (e.g., hitting the ball hard) and how they were more within one's control than outcome goals (e.g., hitting .300). Emphasis was then placed on consistency—in order to hit the ball hard consistently, the players needed to get the fat part of the bat on the ball, and in order to do this, they needed to see the ball well, be in control of themselves, and play the game one pitch at a time. Goals were reworked to focus more on process.

When discussing goal-setting, it's recommended that players and coaches set outcome goals at the beginning of the season but spend 99% of their time on the process and what they can do on each individual day to help reach the desired goal. If this present focus is adopted, the athlete will be doing quality work on an incremental basis and will gain confidence from this preparation.

Discussion with the Cape athletes also emphasized having a focal point that the athletes could use if they felt like they were losing focus or experiencing self-doubts.

Finally, they needed to have a plan and trust it. ***Each athlete's plan came from his preparation and awareness of the situation.*** They have to know what they are trying to do with the pitch at the present moment. Once a plan was in place, the athlete can shift their thoughts to trusting their preparation and focus on performance.

To help with this task, the athletes used swing thoughts such as "see the ball, hit the ball" or "backside, backside, backside." ***The key here was to use a term that freed their minds from over-analyzing the situation and allow them to trust their ability to carry out the plan.***

WORKING THE PROCESS AND QUALITY AT-BAT CARDS

Failure at the plate was ever-present during the 2001 season. That summer the CCBL established all-time lows for League ERA (2.69) and batting average (.224), and an all-time high for strikeouts (3,604). In my role as a mental conditioning coach, I was able to witness the frustration and pressure that so many of the players were experiencing for the first time.

When you're accustomed to hitting between .350 and .400

and all of a sudden you're hitting .220, every time you go to the plate it feels like a matter of life and death. You want to show the scouts, coaches, and everyone that you belong. That summer was the first time ever that most of the players had not hit over .300. They started to question their ability. They were thinking things like, "What am I doing here? I suck. I have been waiting my whole life to play in the Cape and I am embarrassing myself."

Many of the players, like the one quoted above, fell into the trap of judging their performance by end results. The modified goals previously discussed, however, began to steer them in the positive direction of evaluating the process and not the performance. *Teaching athletes to work the process gives them the best chance to be successful and get the desired outcome.* Learning to evaluate themselves on things that they have control over (the process) helps to establish control.

As previously stated, having a clear plan and being able to trust that plan all begins with self-control. Players who were batting anywhere from .120-.260 were quite receptive to evaluating their success on something other than outcome results, such as base hits or batting average. To help them with this performance evaluation, the players were encouraged to complete quality at-bat cards after each game. The cards asked questions related to the process of hitting, such as, whether the player was in control of himself, if he stuck to the plan he took to the plate, how well he saw the ball, and the type of contact he made. The cards provided a concrete way for the players to see that they were working the process, and thus giving themselves the best chance to be successful.

Initially, players saw using the evaluation cards as kind of a pain, because filling them out was the last thing the players wanted to do after a game they lost and didn't get any hits. However, once they realized it only took only a minute and once they established this as a part of their routine, they started to realize that they could do everything right and still go 0-for-5. *Changing their goal from hitting .300 to being in control of themselves, seeing the ball, and giving themselves the best chance for success made sense and reduced the stress of having to get 3-4 hits every day to raise their batting averages.*

By evaluating their process, the players began to have a better understanding of how they could go 0-for-5 and yet still be successful if they were in control of themselves, had a plan, saw the ball well, and made solid contact. They were giving themselves the best chance for success by sticking with the process that enables them to hit the ball hard. Anything beyond the process is out of their control.

PERSONALIZING PERFORMANCE AND SEGMENTATION

When hitting failure occurred, many players struggled not only on the field, but in their personal lives as well. This phenomenon is known as personalizing one's performance.

In my work, I have seen many players correlate the outcome of their performance with their self-perception. When the player performs well, he sees himself as successful; when the player does not, he views himself as a failure. It's this roller-coaster ride that turns many players from prospect into suspect and affects them and their relationships outside of baseball.

Mental Conditioning Coaches often handle athletes who

link their self-worth to performance by implementing a technique known as segmentation—the ability to separate one aspect of life/performance from another. An example of segmentation often talked about by coaches is separating hitting from fielding, i.e., leaving a poor at-bat in the dugout, so it doesn't affect your defensive play; or leaving your personal stuff outside the lines so, it doesn't influence your practice or game performance. Though this technique may sound easy to understand, it can be very difficult to implement.

Segmentation gives the player a physical tool to use to help separate the many different hats they wear. Leaving baseball at the park is much easier said than done, largely due to the levels of commitment these players have given to the game. Many have dedicated their lives to it. This is why it is so important for athletes to establish a routine that enables them to stay more in the present moment when dealing with friends, family, media, or whatever it is the player does outside of baseball.

A technique often used is the changing of ones clothes. When you change your clothes, you can use that physical exercise as a way to let go of anything that is causing mental stress. Remembering that *baseball is what I do it is not who I am* is a key part of keeping your perspective in order and will help set the foundation for successful segmentation.

Another technique that a Cape player found successful was to bang the dirt off his spikes after the game before he left the dugout. He associated that act with banging away the performance, both good and bad, which helped him to leave it at the yard. No matter how he played, he knew that he would have to start over with the score 0-0 the next day.

Another Cape player said that he would start transforming himself into the ultimate baseball player by taking a shower before he got changed to go to the park, leaving his personal life and work in the shower and washing away anything and everything except what he was going to do in that day's baseball game. He would then take another shower after the game, washing away his performance, good or bad, and pick up his personal life and job that he had left before the game.

It's critical that each athlete come up with his own technique(s) for segmentation. Each athlete is different—what works for one may not work for another. *Segmentation needs to be an individual routine that the athlete feels will work for him.*

KEY POINTS FOR REVIEW:

- Having a players' goals written down makes it easier to communicate about what kind of knowledge the player had regarding goal-setting, outcome vs. process goals, expectations, and what type of mental conditioning the player had been exposed to at his school's program.

- Each athlete's plan came from his preparation and awareness of the situation.

- Teaching athletes to work the process gives them the best chance to be successful and get the desired outcome.

- Changing their goal from hitting .300 to being in control of themselves, seeing the ball, and giving themselves the best chance for success made sense and reduced the stress of having to get 3-4 hits every day to raise their batting averages.

- When hitting failure occurs, many players struggle not only on the field, but in their personal lives as well. This phenomenon is known as personalizing one's performance.

- A baseball player must acknowledge this: Baseball is what I do, it is not who I am.

- Segmentation needs to be an individual routine that the athlete feels will work for him.

Chapter 18 | DEVELOPING A LEADERSHIP COUNCIL

Leadership Group Essential for Teaching Future Leaders of Your Program

Communication and teamwork are essential to the success of any organization. Getting players to take ownership of the team, police themselves, and hold each other accountable doesn't just happen. It's a process and a culture that you as the head coach need to take pride in and work to achieve every day.

Many coaches value the relationships they have with players. Battling in the trenches with young men and seeing them mature as they go through the program is one of the greatest joys in coaching. A trap that many coaches fall into is that they get so hung up on winning the national or state championship that they forget the fact that winning is a by-product of doing things the right way on a daily basis and striving for excellence.

An effective way to enhance and improve coach-player, player-coach, and player-player communication is to establish a leadership council. There are many different ways to run a leadership council and many different benefits. In this chapter we will focus on a few things you can do to get started. Remember, it's the start that stops most people and K-A=0 (Knowledge minus Action gets you nothing.) If you believe improving communication in your program will help you come one step closer to achieving excellence, try implementing a leadership council.

SET A SCHEDULE OF MEETING DATES

Setting a scheduled meeting time when you and the council can get together is essential. As a coach, you get pulled in many different directions, often at the last minute. Remember that your number-one priority is the young men whom you brought on campus and are leading at this time. If you prioritize your leadership-council meetings and make a point to be there, it sends a loud and strong message that this is something very important to the success of your program. Most college programs have Monday off, so holding these meetings on a Monday or a Tuesday morning can be the optimal time.

HAVE FOOD, WILL TALK

"Have food, will talk" is an effective motto with today's athletes. If you want your athletes to feel welcome and make it a less formal, more informative open session, try taking your council to lunch or breakfast and see how comfortable they will be.

GET OUT OF YOUR OFFICE

When players come into your office they can be intimidated because you sit behind the big desk and have an aura of power (which you want to keep). Meet with the council in the stands of the stadium, or a luxury box, classroom, dining hall, team room, locker room, classroom or anywhere that you can think of that allows you to be more approachable and less intimidating. When you need to drop the hammer, you bring people in your office and shut the door. When you approach your players to get their opinions on team matters, you want to be in a more neutral, less authoritarian place. The Knights of the Roundtable met at a round table so that each would have an equal voice. Use this strategy to your advantage.

COMPOSITION OF THE COUNCIL

Often you look for the right four or five guys who can commit on a consistent basis. These are the guys that you feel have a good sense of the team and will also be able to look you in the eye and tell you what they feel is going on without fear of retribution. You want guys who will tell you what's on their mind when you ask for it, but also have the understanding that they need to do that in an environment where you ask for it, and not in front of the team.

Often council members can be captains, but they don't need to be. They can be seniors or a mix of upper and underclassmen. You may want to have the team and your coaches vote, use an application and interview process or may want to hand pick them or best case scenario, have the selection process be a combination of the above.

Many coaches also have a rotating ghost chair. The ghost chair is for a player who is not on the council but shows potential leadership capabilities and may have a chance to be on the council in the future. The person in the ghost chair is not allowed to speak; they are there as a fly on the wall and an observer to the process of how things work and what they may be called on to do in the future. Not every meeting has to use the ghost chair, and the council can ask the ghost to leave the meeting if issues need to be discussed between the council and the coach.

GREAT COACHES ARE GREAT LISTENERS

As a coach, pride yourself on being a great listener. Start your meeting by reviewing the purpose of the meeting and that you welcome them to speak what's on their mind. Encourage them to be open and honest with you. Value their input. You want to know what is going on with the team and whether they think the coaches are doing anything they might be able to improve. Maybe players feel like you tighten up when the game gets close, or start to press when you get into a pressure situation. Welcoming this feedback and communication from your players takes a SPECIAL COACH, someone who can put his EGO aside and say, "I do not know everything. I value your input and want to know what you have to say. We are in this together and I am here to support you and help us all achieve collective excellence."

A technique that is most effective for opening up communication lines with your players is to do five or ten minutes of active listening. Let your players know that in this period you WILL NOT BE SPEAKING AT ALL, that YOU CANNOT SPEAK, that you will be listening actively and taking notes for 5-10 minutes. This allows us as coaches not to have to think about an answer or what we might say, it frees us up just to listen at a level of excellence.

Many head coaches are type-A personalities and get very excited when talking about their program and the game of baseball. Unknowingly, they have a tendency to dominate the conversation, and often fail to truly hear what is going on. For some of you, making a commitment to LISTEN for five to ten minutes will be like nothing you have ever experienced. If the players run out of things to say, sit there in silence for the rest of the time. It's amazing how many times you have to sit in silence for eight or nine minutes before the REALLY BIG ELEPHANT IN THE ROOM comes out. Be disciplined and wait the pre-determined amount of time before you speak. BE A GREAT LISTENER.

WHAT I HEARD YOU SAY

After listening for the pre-determined time and taking notes and/or eating lunch, come back with, "Here is what I heard you guys say. Did I get it all or am I missing something?" By letting them know what you heard them say and asking them if that is accurate, you check for understanding to see if what you heard is what they wanted you to hear. Sometimes they will say, "Coach, that's not really what we meant, what we meant was this..." Asking and checking for understanding assures that you get the real message and that you are on the same page. More importantly, it assures your players that you are invested in them and the success of the team.

BENEFITS OF COUNCIL

There are many benefits of running a leadership council. You can develop better relationships with your players, improve communication between players and coaches, and have a greater understanding of the team's perspective and potential team issues that you may not be aware of otherwise.

If you're dedicated enough to have read this far, I believe you are a coach that is in the pursuit of excellence. Finding a way to improve the communication in your program, as well as finding a way to hear things from the players' perspective, will give you a far greater feel for the state of your team and allow you to be more proactive with coaching for chemistry and communication. Take the time to step back and be an excellent listener. Take the time to hear things from your players' perspective. Leadership is a skill. Coach it just like you do the physical fundamentals of your sport.

Team chemistry is TRUST, trust between players, trust that the coaches have for players, and trust that players have for coaches. Everyone has to earn it. As a coach you can't just walk through the door and expect the kids to TRUST you and the other coaches because of a resume. Trust must be earned by how you communicate, how you prepare, how you conduct yourself. All of these actions should improve the athletes' level of trust in you as their leader.

STUDENT-ATHLETE SHARES LEADERSHIP INSIGHT

The following is from an essay about leadership written by a high-school student-athlete applying to be on their teams leadership council.

"It goes without question that good leadership is necessary for any team. But what makes good leadership? What makes a good leader? Leadership is a choice. It's not a status or rank, it's a trait inside everybody. It's personal. Leadership is something obtained through an individual's ethics, desire, intentions, and, most importantly, their daily actions. A good leader recognizes that commitment, communication, honesty, and trust are all important in guiding the team to success.

I believe there are some skills essential for every leader

to be respected and effective. One must lead by example, displaying a confidence that becomes contagious. With a confident composure and positive attitude, you can inspire others to see what they are capable of and unlock their individual potential. Leaders have the courage and determination to accomplish a goal, regardless of the seemingly impossible obstacles. Leadership is the ability to make the team members believe in each other, enabling the team to accomplish what individuals cannot do on their own.

The best way to learn how to be a leader is through experience. At the 2004 International Children's Games in Cleveland, I experienced leadership; discovering you didn't need to be the oldest, the most popular, or even the most skilled player to lead a team. My desire to win became contagious, my extraordinarily high expectations for success became the team's expectations, and my all-out effort and positive mind-set became that of the team. Over 3,000 athletes representing fifty different countries from around the world gathered to compete and there was no doubt that every athlete there, including myself, felt some fear of failure, a fear of not succeeding. The strength to overcome that fear is what made the leaders of their teams and representatives of their nations rise above the rest. I learned that leaders aren't diminished by fear; they are motivated and ever changed by it.

There is leadership ability inside everyone—whether you are the captain of a twenty-six-time world championship team, or a fourteen-year-old girl experiencing the role for the first time. Experience is part of what makes a person a leader. At the end of the day, however, leadership is an attitude. It's a way of thinking that you can extend beyond yourself to influence others. It's an attitude you either choose to bring or not. Good leaders are mirrors for their teammates. reflecting the best of what is inside all of us."

KEY POINTS FOR REVIEW:

• **Leadership councils are a way of improving coach-player and player-player relationships and communication.**

• **Select four or five players who have a sense of what is going on and the confidence to speak openly without fear of retribution.**

• **Set a scheduled meeting time and place outside of the coach's office and stick to it.**

• **The coach must listen carefully and repeat back what he has heard to make sure he understands it.**

Visit www.SoWhatNextPitch.com/EXTRAS
For BONUS Mental Conditioning Material &
FREE Peak Performance Training Tools

Chapter 19 | BASE 2:
YOUR STRATEGY FOR SUCCESS

An In-Game Strategy that Wins

Coaches often look for simple-to-use systems that can be consistent offensively and defensively, as well as off the field and in the community and classroom. I believe that BASE 2 provides a simple-to-use system that can be the foundation for your program's success.

B=BIG INNING

Offensively, the "big inning" is scoring three or more runs in a single inning. When you do that, you dramatically increase your chance of being rewarded with a victory. Defensively, if you can prevent the other team from putting up a three run or greater inning, you will most likely keep your team in the game long enough to have a chance at the end.

I consider the big inning in the community to be getting involved in that one big event that helps your program earn the respect of fans and community members. An example would be a program doing a green-up day, in which they go to a local city park and clean up garbage, paint picnic tables, and help make the area a safer place for kids in the community.

Academically, the big inning is taking advantage of extra-academic opportunities that are available. This could manifest in players attending extra-help sessions and/or the team collectively attending guest lectures on campus. This is doing the things that some may see as extra, but you see as a way to give yourself the best chance for success. *It takes no talent to show up to class and to take advantage of extra educational opportunities.*

A=ANSWER BACK

Offensively, we know it's important when the other team scores to answer back at the next opportunity. Gaining back the momentum, and getting up off the canvas when you have been knocked down, sends a strong message that you're here to play, and play to win. Answering back is a sign of a championship team.

Defensively, answering back after you score on offense is keeping your opponent off the scoreboard with a shutdown inning. A pitcher who can come out and pound the strike zone, aggressively force contact, and pitch with a good rhythm gives the defense the best chance to hang a zero. Keeping your opponent at bay after you score can be a huge momentum swing in your direction.

The answer-back in the community is constantly doing things to help your program and school have a good name. It's inevitable for people to make mistakes. Bad decisions, unfortunately, are made all the time. A coach may get behind the wheel of his car after having a few drinks or a student may decide to walk out of a restaurant without paying for a meal. *Whatever the infraction, the RESPONSE, or the answer-back, when faced with adversity is what defines you.*

We talk a lot about *E+R=O. Event plus Response equals Outcome.* It's not the event or the mistakes (a bad outing or losing a game) that define us and determine our outcome. It's the response to those events that ultimately determines who and what we become.

The answer-back in school is symbolic of a student-athlete approaching their teacher after receiving a graded paper or exam and seeking the necessary assistance to improve their grade and their knowledge of the course material. Learning how to take tests and write is as important as the content knowledge you demonstrate while taking the exam or writing the paper. Learning what you did incorrectly in the process will help improve you performance in the future.

S=SCORE FIRST

Offensively, scoring the first run of the game sets the tone for the rest of the game. Statistically speaking, the team that scores first usually wins.

Defensively, if you can prevent the other team from getting on the scoreboard first, you're giving your team the advantage not only in statistical winning percentage but also in momentum and confidence. If you can prevent the other team from scoring in the first inning, usually your pitcher will have a better chance of keeping the game close. We all know how pitchers can struggle in that first inning, but find it in the second and get on a roll.

In the community, scoring first is being the first one to sign up for an opportunity to give back. It's being the first team to volunteer to go to the elementary school and read to children. It's being the first team at the dorms on move-in day for freshmen, helping other students ease into their first day of college by helping them get their belongings from their car and into their dorm.

In school, scoring first is sitting in the front row of class. It's knowing your professors' names and making sure they know who you are. It's stopping by the office of your teachers on a routine basis just to say hello so you know for certain that they know who you are, and not just a baseball player with student ID #12345.

E=EXTEND THE LEAD

Extending the lead that you have on the offensive side of the game is critical to putting teams away and surviving that late-inning comeback. Extending the lead is about putting your opponent out when you have them on the ropes. It's not resting comfortably and contently with the scoreboard in your favor, it's the relentless pursuit of more runs and widening the gap between you and the other team.

Defensively, we want to prevent the other team from extending the lead. When we are down, we want to do whatever we must to keep the game close until our offense finds a way to get us back on the positive side of the scoreboard.

Extending the lead in the community is bringing back former players who have been successful in your program and who are now successful in the community and having them speak to the current team about how the things the athletes are learning in baseball will provide a solid foundation for future success. Extending the lead can be inviting successful people in your community to speak to your team in a "successful speakers series" format about what it takes to succeed in life after baseball.

Extending the lead in the classroom is finding a way to surround yourself with people who are academically more gifted or more disciplined than you are. *When you surround yourself with people who get better grades than you do and with people who have better studying habits than you do, ultimately you will start to do the things that they do and become more successful.* Having a team study period or inviting in tutors or other students as a part of your team study table will help foster an extending-the-lead mentality in the classroom.

2 = TWO-OUT PERFORMANCE, TWO-OUT RBI

Offensively, if you score runs with two outs, you will find that you take the wind out of the other team's sails. Two-out RBIs can become big innings and are definitely momentum-turning moments.

Defensively, if you can keep the other team from scoring runs with two outs, you will prevent most big innings and get your team back in the dugout where they want to be.

The two-out performance in the community is finding a way to come through in the clutch when the pressure is on. One example is having the awareness to remove yourself from a potentially negative situation, such as being at an underage party and leaving when the alcohol shows up because you signed a code of conduct that says "I will not participate in underage drinking." Likewise, *a two-out clutch performance could be getting one of your intoxicated teammates out of a potentially negative situation and into a safer environment before something disastrous happens.*

The two-out clutch performance in school is making sure you grind it out until the end of the semester and show up for exams. It's all too common for students to show up to class, do all the assignments, do okay on tests, and then bomb the final exam by failing to prepare. Clutch performances in academics are preparing enough to nail the presentation, getting the paper done early so you can get feedback from the writing center, and by all means making sure you do your own work and never giving in to the temptation to cheat, because your integrity and learning is more important than grades.

BASE 2 can be tweaked to cover anything you feel is important in an academic or community setting. I feel it can serve as a great tool for performance evaluation over the course of a season. Try keeping a chart like the one below and see if there is a correlation between your ability to achieve BASE 2 on the offensive side of the game and your winning percentage.

	Game 1	Game 2	Game 3	Game 4	Game 5	Game 6	Game 7	Game 8
B								
A								
S								
E								
2								
W/L								

STOPWATCH TIMES YOU WANT TO KEEP

You can also keep track of your pitchers' time on the field and time in the dugout, similar to what football teams do with time of possession. *Win the battle of having your pitcher in the dugout more, win the time of possession, and see how that affects the game.*

You can also put a stopwatch on your infield and outfield pre-game and see how quickly you can go through your routine without rushing – remember, *be quick, but don't hurry. Play fast, have fun, and play one pitch at a time.*

KEY POINTS FOR REVIEW:

- It takes no talent to show up to class and to take advantage of extra help opportunities.

- Whatever the infraction, the RESPONSE, or the answer-back, when faced with adversity, is what defines you.

- When you surround yourself with people who get better grades than you do and with people who have better studying habits than you do, ultimately you will start to do the things that they do and become more successful.

- Extending the lead in the community is bringing back former players who have been successful in your program and are now successful in the community, and having them speak to the current team about how the things the athletes are learning in baseball will provide a solid foundation for future success.

- A two-out clutch performance could be getting one of your intoxicated teammates out of a potentially negative situation and into a safer environment before something disastrous happens.

- Be quick but don't hurry. Play fast, have fun, and play one pitch at a time.

Visit www.SoWhatNextPitch.com/EXTRAS
For BONUS Mental Conditioning Material &
FREE Peak Performance Training Tools

Chapter 20 | USING VELOCITY SIMULATION AND ROUTINES TO INCREASE THE EFFECTIVENESS OF BATTING PRACTICE

Trying to find ways to make practice more game-like is one of the biggest challenges baseball coaches face. Simulating the velocity of the starting pitcher you will face is easier than most people think and will help you to have a more game-like batting practice.

VELOCITY-SIMULATED BATTING PRACTICE

With the advantage of detailed scouting reports, a technique that great coaches use is velocity-simulated batting practice. In this form of practice, the batting-practice pitcher is a specific distance from the hitter to mimic the timing they will need on game day. A simple formula can be implemented to give hitters a more game-like and realistic batting practice experience.

Plugging numbers into the right mathematical equation can simulate the pitching speed that a team will face in a game during batting practice. Teams have used this formula and had great success with their hitters being more prepared to face the starting pitcher. After utilizing velocity-simulated batting practices, hitters have been more on time and had more quality at-bats early in the game because they have felt more prepared.

VELOCITY-SIMULATION EQUATION

The velocity-simulation equation is A over B equals C over D. By cross multiplying A and D, and then dividing by B, you are able to come up with C, which is the number of feet from which you want to be throwing during a pre-game batting practice.

A   C
– X –
B   D

A = Mound distance from home plate –
    60 feet, 6 inches

B = Radar gun MPH of starting pitcher you will face

C = Feet from hitter batting-practice pitcher should
    be to simulate starting pitcher velocity.

D = Batting-practice pitchers' MPH of batting-
    practice pitches

For example, if you will be facing a pitcher who has a 98 MPH fastball and your batting-practice pitching speed is 45 MPH, you multiply 60.5 (A) (we use .5 as in sixty and one-half feet) and 45 (D) and then divide your answer by 98 (B) to get the number of feet from which you need to throw batting practice, which in this case is 27.8 feet (C).

If you will be facing a 92 MPH pitcher and your batting-practice pitcher throws 51 MPH, you would multiply 60.5 x 51 (3085.5) and divide by 92, which comes to 33.54 feet. That's the distance from home plate your BP pitcher should be to simulate a 92-MPH fastball by throwing 51 MPH.

TAKE ADVANTAGE OF STATIONS AND MACHINES

Setting up your pre-game batting practice to mimic and simulate the pitcher you will be facing in your next game is a simple way to help you prepare. If you're facing a curveball pitcher, set up a pitching machine to throw "Uncle Charlie" so your players can get used to seeing the break of the ball.

Setting up stations in your batting-practice routine is also a great way to get more game-like swings into your preparation.

Rather than have a player get in the cage and take 10 swings in a row, a more game-like routine would be to divide your team into groups and use stations. Rather than taking 10 swings in a row, which is unlikely to happen in a game, take two rounds of five swings or three rounds of four swings, which accurately simulates a game at-bat. Having a machine station where you can bunt a good fastball or breaking pitch will also allow you to focus more on hitting on the main diamond and get more quality repetitions at a specific station.

Using base-running stations in batting practice so players can read the down angle of the ball off the bat from third base or the pitch down in the dirt from first base are good ways to get the players' base-running mentality in check.

KEY POINTS FOR REVIEW:

• With the advantage of detailed scouting reports, a technique great coaches use to prepare their pitchers is velocity-simulated batting practice.

• Plugging numbers into the right mathematical equation can simulate the pitching speed that batters will face in the game during batting practice.

• Setting up stations in your batting-practice routine is also a great way to get more game-like swings into your preparation.

Chapter 21 | PERSPECTIVE IS REALITY

Choosing Your Perspective
Essential In A Game of Failure

Baseball is a game of failure; this we all know. How to handle failure; this we all need to know better. As a Mental Conditioning Coach for some of the top college and high school baseball programs in the country (8 of the top 25 ranked teams in NCAA Div. I as of March 8, 2012) and formerly with the Washington Nationals, I want to share some simple yet powerful perspective on handling failure that has helped the teams, coaches, and players I am blessed to work with.

PERPECTIVE IS REALITY

As human beings our perspective is our reality. The way you see things is the way they are… TO YOU. How is it that two players in the same situation can perform at two opposite sides of the spectrum? My experience has indicated that pressure can be magnified or nullified by perspective.

BEST TEAM NEVER WINS

Having worked with 7 college baseball teams in 2007 and three that went to the post-season, I would have said the talent at UC Irvine in 2007 was not better than the other two teams in the field that year including #1 National Seed Vanderbilt. From a perspective standpoint, there were as good as anyone in the country. They realized that the best team never wins, it's the team that plays the best that wins and their focus was 100% on what they needed to do to play at their best and win pitches.

FRUSTRATED OR FASCINATED

Getting frustrated or fascinated with adversity is a matter of perspective. Getting turned on and working smarter and harder or getting turned off and tapping out or quitting is a matter of perspective. Dave Serrano the head baseball coach at The University of Tennessee who lead UC Irvine to Omaha in 2007 said it best in his press conference when hired at UT. Serrano talked about creating a culture of will over skill and controlling what you can control. He is talking about perspective. He is talking about mental toughness.

WHAT IS vs. WHAT IF

Working with Ultimate Fighting Championship Welterweight World Champion Georges St. Pierre, currently rehabilitating an injury, will defend his title vs. Carlos Condit in the fall of 2012, I was impressed with his focus on What Is (rehab) as opposed to What If (defending his title months down the road). Many of us can fall into the trap of thinking about what if this happens, what if that happens and we pull ourselves out of the present and pull ourselves away from what is.

St. Pierre is able to focus one day at a time and on (WIN) What's Important Now – his rehabilitation, not fighting. That's where he needs to be mentally because that is where he is at physically. As baseball players, we often are in the batter's box or on the mound and thinking about what might happen in the future or worse what has happened in the past vs. what is in the NOW. Choose to take the perspective of What Is versus What If.

ACCEPT vs. FORGET ABOUT

Eric Backich, head baseball coach at The University of Maryland who has had the Terrapins in the CBN top 25 for the first time since the 1980's, talks about the difference between accepting what the game has to offer versus forgetting about the past.

"You must accept that the game is going to be challenging, you must accept and take responsibility for your previous good and bad performances and you must accept that you are not going to be perfect. When you do that, you remove the mental emergency break and allow yourself to be free from the negativity. Choose to accept that this is a HARD game and you will fail more that you will succeed. ACCEPT IT!"

EXCELLENT vs. PERFECT

The best coaches I have been blessed to work with from George Horton at Cal State Fullerton (2004 National Champions), Pat Casey at Oregon State (2006 & 2007 National Champions) , Tim Corbin at Vanderbilt (2011 CWS) and Jim Schlossnagle at TCU (2010 CWS) at the collegiate level and guys like Ron Eastman from The Woodlands HS in Texas (2006 National Champions) and Joe Sato at Bingham HS in Utah (CBN Top 25 HS Baseball Program) talk more about excellence and the process of winning than they do about winning itself. They also stress to their athletes that practice makes permanent, not perfect.

Perfection is unattainable. The pursuit of excellence mandates that you are going to get kicked in the teeth, knocked down and spit on. Fans, parents, media and administration can be fickle and they will love you when you win and criticize you when you lose. Understanding that you are pursuing excellence, and that the pursuit of excellence has no finish line, will allow you to accept that you are going to play good and bad. This pursuit of excellence allows you to accept that your goal is to play as well as you can as often as you can, competing against yourself and the game. This pursuit of excellence allows you to focus on the process and let the results, which are out of your control, take care of itself. Perfection leads to playing not to lose, while the pursuit of excellence gives you the best chance to win.

GOOD & BAD vs. GOOD OR BAD

Mike Bianco, the head baseball coach for 2009 SEC Champion Ole Miss says that when you can evaluate your performance as good and bad instead of good or bad you will be more consistent mentally and emotionally and give yourself a better chance to play at a high level.

Deciding, before you compete that, you are going to evaluate your performance as good and bad versus good or bad is allowing you to accept the fact that you are not going to be perfect and that you are going to have some success and some adversity. Most importantly, by adopting this perspective you choose to evaluate your performance from the perspective of a learner in order to find information to help you get better and to evaluate your performance with less emotion and more matter of fact.

Emotion clouds reality, and when you can remove emotion from your lens of perception and see more of what is and less of what if (future thinking outside the moment) you will see more of the TRUE picture. Choose to accept that the reality of events will always be good and bad, and stop evaluating them as solely good or bad.

LOSER OR LEARNER

When you lose a game, does that make you a loser? Can a loss be something that helps you to get to another level? Ty Harrington the head baseball coach at Texas State University led the Bobcats into the CBN top 25 and in 2011 took the Bobcats to the Southland Conference Tournament Championship after losing their first game of the tournament.

He has instilled in his team, when faced with losing a game, the capability to not lose the message and to retain the game's lessons. In the pursuit of excellence, his teams have learned to ascertain the valuable information hidden within each loss and apply it to the process of team improvement. This is a skill all teams should be attempting to master.

Similarly, Georges St. Pierre says that the best thing that ever happened to him was losing his World Championship to Matt Serra in April of 2007. As an athlete, you must make the choice when you lose to perceive the loss as a lesson from which you can learn and improve. Choose to be a learner.

BITTER OR BETTER

Todd Whitting, head baseball coach at The University of Houston recently said something that stuck with me. He had been speaking to his team after a tough loss in a game where they had the bases loaded down by one with one out in the 9th inning and could not get the necessary run across. In his post-game speech, he challenged his team to get better, not bitter.

Coach Whitting challenged his players to make a choice. As a team, they needed to decide whether they were going to allow this loss or a lack of playing time or a lack of personal and team success to make them bitter toward the game of baseball or whether this loss would act as fuel to make them better. He said that if the team was going to move forward together, they had to get encouraged, not discouraged, by this experience and collectively choose to learn from this adversity.

As a team, Whitting and the Cougars chose to use the loss as a lesson and a few days later found success in their victories over Southeastern Conference powers The University of Tennessee and #4 ranked University of Arkansas at Minute Maid Stadium in Houston.

THE LESSON FROM THE BOLL WEEVIL

Most people think that adversity is a negative thing. That life is better when things are going well. What people often fail to remember is that tough times don't last, tough people do.

The year was 1915, and the location was Enterprise, Alabama. The major source of commerce and income in Enterprise was the abundance of cotton crops and was a world leader in cotton production. However by 1918, a small insect, about the size of your thumb, had appeared and was wreaking havoc on Enterprise and their cotton crop.

The boll weevil a, small insect indigenous to Mexico, had

appeared in Alabama in 1915 and by 1918 farmers were losing whole cotton crops to the beetle. H. M. Sessions saw this agricultural devastation as an opportunity to convert the area to peanut farming and in 1916 he convinced C. W. Baston, an indebted farmer, to back his venture.

The first crop of peanuts paid off their debts, and a large portion of the crop was bought by other farmers seeking to make a transition to peanut farming. Cotton was grown again, but farmers soon learned to diversify their crops, a practice which brought new money to Coffee County, Alabama and the city of Enterprise.

Bon Fleming, a local businessman, came up with the idea to build a monument, as a tribute to the Boll Weevil and let it serve as a constant reminder of how something disastrous can be a catalyst for change, and a reminder of how the people of Enterprise adjusted in the face of adversity. The monument was dedicated on December 11, 1919 at the intersection of College and Main Street, the heart of the town's business district.

At the base of the monument appears the following inscription "In profound appreciation of the Boll Weevil and what it has done as the herald of prosperity this monument was erected by the citizens of Enterprise, Coffee County, Alabama."

The monument was built to show their appreciation to an insect, the boll weevil, for its profound influence on the area's agriculture and economy. Hailing the beetle as a "herald of prosperity," it stands as the world's only monument built to honor an agricultural pest. In April, 1973, the monument was added to the National Registry of Historic Places.

Today, you have the opportunity to take one of your greatest adversities, and turn it into your greatest gift. Remember that every setback sets the stage for your greatest comeback. Today, embrace adversity, welcome the challenge of a great opponent, and play your game, one pitch at a time.

FAILURE IS POSITIVE FEEDBACK

My mentor Dr. Ken Ravizza taught us that failure was unavoidable in the pursuit of excellence, and that failure was healthy and not to be avoided but embraced, because failure gives you an opportunity to learn and to grow. Without failure, we are without progress.

If you are like most average people and fear failure or have failed to embrace failure, then I have a fool proof system for you. It will help you win every game. What you need to do is drop out of your competitive league and go play against the local Jr. High B level teams. That is assuming that you are not a Jr. High Coach. If you are a Jr. High coach reading this, you must go play the little league teams in your area. When you play that schedule you will win. But you will also not have much fun.

Augie Garrido the head coach at The University of Texas speaks of failure as an unavoidable part of the game and as failure as a true competitor's friend. We all enjoy our success in the game, but the only reason we enjoy the success is because there is so much failure. Failure is not negative, it is positive. It means you are competing at the right level and it means that you have an opportunity to learn and use that failure as positive feedback. Make the choice to compete. Learn and grow from your failures.

BASEBALL IS WHAT YOU DO, NOT WHO YOU ARE

One of the most mentally tough pitchers in college baseball I have worked with was Matt Purke at Texas Christian University in 2010 and 2011. After being selected in the 1st round of the MLB Draft by the Texas Rangers, Purke went to TCU to play for a master of the mental game in Jim Schlossnagle. Purke put up one of the best seasons in the history of college baseball... as a freshman. The left handed pitcher was 16-0. What was more impressive was how he handled the success and also how he handled adversity in his sophomore season.

Purke said that he was able to stay humble and hungry by keeping the perspective that baseball was what he did, not who he was. Purke was not defined by his performance. He did not take his performance personally and treat you differently if he won versus if he lost. He was a true professional, mature well ahead of his years. He was also one of the most competitive players I have ever worked with.

Do not let the success or failure of your on-field performance dictate how you treat others and how you view yourself. Personalizing performance is a trap that will suck you in, beat you up, and spit you out the other side a non-consistent competitor.

KEY POINTS FOR REVIEW:

• **Perspective is reality. The way you see things is the way they are for you. That does not mean that others see your situation the same way you do.**

• **The best team never wins, it is always the team that plays the best.**

• **Failure is positive feedback. You can learn a lot from failure. You must choose to be a learner, not a loser, to get better, not bitter when faced with adversity and challenge.**

• **You choose to get frustrated or fascinated in the face of adversity.**

• **Choose to focus on what is and let go of what if. When you focus on what is you are living in the present, when you focus on what if, you are living with one foot in the past and one foot in the future.**

• **You can not forget about what has happened in the past. Accept that you are not perfect, that you will make mistakes, learn from them and move on.**

• **Choose to try and be excellent rather than try to be perfect. Being perfect is unattainable, being excellent is about your ability to handle adversity.**

• **Refuse to evaluate your performance as good or bad and choose to see it as good and bad.**

• **What is your Boll Weevil?**

• **Baseball is what you do, not who you are. Keep the game in perspective.**

Chapter 22 | HOW TO DEVELOP CHAMPIONSHIP TEAM CHEMISTRY

Developing A Team Mission Statement

Have you ever been a part of a team that had a lot of individual talent, but underachieved? You probably lost games you thought you should have won, and didn't have as much fun playing.

Have you ever been a part of a team that didn't have a lot of individual talent, but overachieved? You probably won a lot of games and had a ton of fun being with your teammates on and off the field.

If you have experienced either of these two situations, you know firsthand that team chemistry can either take you to the top or drag you to down. Team chemistry is difficult to see, and quantify. Statistics that compare team chemistry do not exist, but developing team chemistry can be part of practice just like working on the fundamentals of your sport. This chapter will provide you with the information necessary to develop a team mission statement that will assure your team have championship team chemistry.

Championship team chemistry is often reported by teams as having a group of people who respect each other and are willing to make personal sacrifices for the good of the team. Championship teams commit to a common goal and often talk about being on a mission. It is often this synergistic atmosphere and attitude that will turn your team into champions.

TEAM SYNERGY

1+1=2, WRONG!!! My Uncle Bud Boucher works on a farm in Vermont, and recently called me to tell me that he just learned a new farming technique. Uncle Bud explained how he would always have only one of his mules plow his field at a time. After about 5 hours the mule would get tired and he would have to switch mules. He worked his mules in these 5 hour shifts for years. However, one day he hooked up two mules to the plow, thinking that they would be able to double their production in only 5 hours time. He was amazed when his mules were able to plow twice as fast and for almost 15 hours, almost three times as long as they could plow on their own.

When I asked him how this had happened, he enthusiastically explained, "The mules were working together very well, and were accomplishing more than either one of them ever had on their own. They got excited at seeing their improved results, became motivated, and just kept on working." My Uncle Bud has never been known as a genius, but that day he experienced synergy. 1+1 = 3 or more.

As an athletic director, performance enhancement consultant, and as a coach at the college, high school and international levels, the teams that have the most success, are the teams that have great synergy. I have found that the best way to create a synergistic environment on athletic teams is by developing a team mission.

ESTABLISHING A TEAM MISSION

A clear mission will minimize the stress that is unavoidable in sports. A mission gives you something to go to when faced with the difficult decisions and temptations of doing something that might not be in the best interest of the team, i.e., going to a party or cheating on an exam. The mission also provides meaning for the team, establishing direction and intensity in your pursuit of excellence. With a team mission, everyone knows why they are getting up early in the morning to go to the weight room and why they are going to bed instead of going out with friends until the early morning hours. A mission provides unified purpose for the team and makes difficult decisions much easier for individual athletes.

The mission must indicate the need for each athlete to give their best effort in all meetings and practices in order to give the team the best chance at accomplishing their collective goals. With this in mind, the mission must also provide a discipline system for the team, clearly outlining the team's goals and objectives, and what they must do to accomplish them. This enables coaches to constantly refer to the team's mission to refocus athletes during team meetings, practice, a bad loss or even a big win. Similarly, players can use the reference the mission to refocus each other, which ultimately establishes improved self-discipline amongst themselves. The beauty of creating a mission is that coaches and players can easily turn to their joint mission to refocus and meet one another on the same level ground.

As aforementioned, one of the most significant benefits of developing a mission statement is the fact that the athletes internalize this mission and take greater ownership of the team. As a result, athletes invest more of themselves into the team and each other. Pat Summit, Head Women's Basketball Coach at The University of Tennessee said it best, "The more responsibility the team is given, the more committed the team will be to a project, and the more they then make it their project. When it's theirs, they feel more accountable for its success or failure, and they do whatever it takes to help it succeed. It becomes "our" team instead of "my" team." This is the power of establishing a team mission.

HOW TO DEVELOP A TEAM MISSION

You will start by dividing the team into equal groups, preferable no more than 5-8 team members per group, and no less than 3-5 groups. You will want to disperse you team leaders and team entertainers so that you have a mixture of players in each group. Give each group a sheet of paper with space for 5 sentences. The group will then work together to develop at least 5 sentences that discuss what the team must do to be successful. Sentences that describe the type of passion, attitude, work ethic, desire, discipline, goals, and expectations on and off the field that the team will need to be successful are often very useful.

The groups will also need to come up with a team theme. The team theme should be a buzzword or a "buzz saying" that will remind the team of their mission, what it means, and that they need to be carrying that out today. The theme is often used on the back of t-shirts or when teams break from huddles for motivational purposes, and as a reminder of their mission. Examples of themes that have been commonly used are "Refuse To Lose", "One Pitch At A Time", "TEAM – Together Everyone Achieves More if there is a Total Effort from All Members", and "No Regrets."

After approximately 10 minutes, or when the groups are

finished writing their sentences and theme, have a member of each group stand up and share their sentences and theme. After each group reads, discuss each of the themes and how it symbolizes what they need to do to be successful. Sometimes the team can agree on a theme very quickly, other times it is best to give it a couple days and see which theme keeps popping up at practices and team interactions.

Collect all the sheets and then take out specific sentences or work together different words from various sentences to produce a paragraph or a list that will explain what it will take for that team to be successful this season. Take your paragraph or list and present it on a big poster or piece of paper that each athlete can sign, and hang this in the locker room or team common area. Also give each athlete a miniature copy of your team mission so they can have a constant reminder of what it is they are committing to and working toward.

The effects of establishing a team mission will be overwhelmingly positive for any team that adopts it the foundation set to achieve a common goal. Developing a team mission statement will increase commitment among athlete's to the team, increase the quality of practices, improve performance in competitions, and elevate the amount of fun and enjoyment found in being a part of a successful organization designed to teach life skills through sport.

KEY POINTS FOR REVIEW:

• Team synergy can be created. When teams have synergy together everyone achieves more if there is a total effort from all members. With synergy 1+1 = 3 or more.

• Developing a team mission statement will help you to get your team on the same page and establish a statement of purpose that will help keep everyone on the same page and provide the foundation from which to grow.

• There is no right or wrong way to develop a team mission statement.

• As a coach, give each athlete a miniature copy of your team mission so they can have a constant reminder of what it is they are committing to and working towards.

Visit www.SoWhatNextPitch.com/EXTRAS
For BONUS Mental Conditioning Material &
FREE Peak Performance Training Tools

Chapter 23 | THE TOP TEN THINGS WORLD CHAMPIONS KNOW THAT YOU DON'T

Cain Shares Quick Tips From Working With World Champions In Various Sports

1. ACTING CHANGES EVERYTHING (ACE)

World champion athletes have an ACE card up their sleeve. That ACE card is a key weapon in their peak performance toolbox. What does ACE stand for? ACE stands for Acting Changes Everything. World champion athletes understand that they're not athletes, they're actors and how they act will greatly impact their performance.

2. FORCE YOURSELF TO ACT DIFFERENT THAN HOW YOU FEEL

It is a lot easier to act yourself into feeling than it is to wait around and feel yourself into action. If you are not confident, that is OK, just act confident. If you are scared, that is OK, just act as if you are not scared. The Karelian Bear Dog chases the grizzly bear not because he's bigger or stronger, but because he believes he's bigger and stronger.

3. LOSING IS NOT AN OPTION

World champions know that losing is not an option, it's essential. In order for you to become a world champion, you're going to lose. You're going to lose because you're competing against the best of the best. And when you get higher and higher in levels of competition, talent and physical skill means less and less because everyone has got it. It's inevitable that you will eventually lose, know how to respond when it happens. Learn from it and move forward. Failure is positive feedback.

4. CONFIDENCE IS A CHOICE

Being a world champion is also about learning how to respond when you are faced with adversity and how to respond when you don't feel good. Do you respond with confidence? Remember, confidence is a choice. World champions don't wake up one day and say, "Hmmm, well the sun and the moon and the stars are all lined up today, so I will be confident". It doesn't work that way with world champions. They make the choice every day to jump out of bed and be confident. They know their 'ABCs' are to 'Always Behave Confidently' because confidence is a choice.

5. THE TEN DEADLY WORDS IN PERFORMANCE

There are ten deadly words that will crush your performance if you say them or believe them. If you're trying to be excellent, if you're trying to get to the top of your field, then paying attention to these ten deadly words will sabotage your career. Those ten deadly words are, "What will other people say? What will other people think?"

What other people say and what other people think are both outside of your control. Thus, it doesn't matter what other people say and it doesn't matter what other people think. In your pursuit of excellence, people are going to try and pull you down and talk trash about you, because you are trying to become better than they are. When people say things about you behind your back or stab you in the back it is because you are in front of them. Be more concerned with your character, what you know is true, than your reputation, what other people say or think about you.

6 CHAMPIONS ARE MADE, THEY'RE NOT BORN

Very few people are truly committed to the pursuit of excellence. Get used to looking yourself in the mirror, questioning your commitment and answering to yourself in the affirmative. Every night, when that head hits the pillow, that's the person you're going to answer to. Other people are going to tell you, you can't do it. That you're not big enough, fast enough or strong enough. Listening to these people and internalizing their negative beliefs is counterproductive to achieving your goals. Don't let these people drag you down, rise above them. Prove them wrong.

The opposite scenario may also be true, which can be equally destructive to your goals. You may be surrounded by a bunch of "yes" people who tell you that you're the best when you are really quite average or just a big fish in a small pond. If you have grand aspirations, you just can't listen to the hype. World champions know it doesn't matter what people think because champions are made – they're developed - they're not born. Champions know there will always be people who have the same goals working just as hard as, if not harder than, they are. ANYONE can be a champion if they are committed to excellence and follow the fundamentals.

7. MOTIVATION IS A DAILY DECISION

To stay motivated, you've got to surround yourself with images, quotes, videos and other visual reminders that will motivate you. Do you have a vision board posted in your office, room, car or locker that shows you what you want to accomplish? This is very much like advertising to yourself what it is you want.

Coke and Pepsi are the two most famous soft drinks in the world and that is largely due to the fact that they saturate the market and your head with advertising. You want to advertise to yourself on a daily basis with vision boards, photos of your next opponent, quotes or goals written on your bathroom mirror with a dry erase marker and by reading a little a lot from good books.

8. YOUR TIME IS NOW!

Your time to DOMINATE IS NOW! Live in the present moment. 1984 Olympic gold medal winning Team USA Hockey Coach Herb Brooks said it best in the great movie "Miracle" when he simply stated with a stern conviction, "Your time is now." The time is now, the place is here. Your career is the sum of your today's. The only factor that is the same amongst all athletes and coaches in the world is that they have 86,000 seconds in a day to either spend or INVEST in the development of their abilities. Maximize your time by having great time management and time prioritization skills and you will get the most out of your potential.

9. DON'T COUNT THE DAYS, MAKE THE DAYS COUNT

World champions also know that you don't count the days till the next fight, but make the days count until then. They set long term goals of where they want to be at the end of the year, but commit 100% to today's goal, to the here and now. They realize that yesterday is history, tomorrow is a mystery and today is a gift, that's why we call it the present. They live for today and get the most out of today because they know their career and life will be the sum of their today's.

10. WHAT'S IMPORTANT NOW (WIN)

What are you going to do today to get better? What is your goal for today? Throughout each day there are going to be distractions, fish hooks that rip you out of the moment while you are pursuing your goals. When you get distracted, recognize it, and refocus in the moment. Winning is an end result that takes care of itself if you win the moment. You win the moment by remembering What's Important Now!

11. BONUS

The BONUS eleventh thing that world champions know that you don't is that the opponent Is You. Your toughest opponent in life will be to master yourself. And once you become a master of your mental game, you give yourself the best chance to become a champion.

KEY POINTS FOR REVIEW:

• Acting changes everything.

• Force yourself to act different than how you feel.

• Losing is not an option.

• Confidence is a choice.

• Know the ten deadly words and watch out for what other people say and what other people think.

• Champions are made, they are not born.

• Motivation is a daily decision.

• Your time is now.

• Don't count the days, make the days count.

• What's Important Now.

• The opponent is you.

Visit www.SoWhatNextPitch.com/EXTRAS
For BONUS Mental Conditioning Material &
FREE Peak Performance Training Tools

PART 4

Concentration Training Grids, Notes, Inner Circle and More...

Chapter 24 | CONCENTRATION GRIDS

Mental Conditioning
One Number at a Time

Concentration grids have been a staple of mental conditioning for years. You are to cross out the numbers 00-99 in order as fast as you can.

You're testing to see how quickly you can perform the task. You're also testing your ability to concentrate. You may play music or do this activity in front of the TV as a way to include distractions. The more you do this activity and the more quickly you can cross out the numbers in order, the more you're developing your ability to concentrate and keep your mind in the present moment

MAJOR LEAGUE MENTAL CONDITIONING

All-Star right-hander Roy Halladay of the Philadelphia Phillies uses it. So do many other professional baseball players and Olympic and professional athletes from various sports to improve their abilities to stay focused and locked-in to the present moment for an extended period of time.

In an April 2007 article by Michael Farber in Sports Illustrated entitled "Second To One," Halladay discussed how he uses the concentration grid as a part of his mental preparation for pitching. He completes the grid twice on the day before he starts and once more on the day he pitches.

The purpose of the exercise is to narrow the focus of a lively mind to nothing but the next number, which helps

Halladay sharpen his concentration on nothing but the next pitch when he reaches the mound.

When Halladay began working the 10-square-by-10-square grid five years ago, he needed 17-20 minutes to finish. Now he has become so proficient that he sometimes amps up the distractions, turning on the TV or listening to songs that he likes. Halladay's average time was reported to be around 3:30.

For years I tried to find a way to recreate this exercise so the athletes I worked with could develop and train their abilities to focus on a routine basis in the comfort of their dorm room or in the discomfort of a local restaurant, dining hall, or sold-out stadium. Recently I was able to develop a computer program that creates a random sequence of 10x10 grids that you can print off your computer and train with on a routine basis.

BENEFITS OF USING CONCENTRATION GRIDS

Athletes I have worked with report that the grids allow them to become more aware of when they start to space out and lose focus. They also allow them to become more aware of when they're trying too hard and need to take a breath in order to relax and get back into an optimal level of focus.

When I personally started doing a "C-Grid" on a routine basis (Monday, Tuesday, Thursday, and Friday mornings before I ate breakfast), my time was in the low to mid teens. After almost two months I was able to do them in about 4-5 minutes, even in the crazy and chaotic environment known as the high-school cafeteria.

USING THE CONCENTRATION GRIDS

When starting out, you want to time your players in a quiet, controlled environment. No cell phone, no TV; no distractions. When performing the grid in a quiet and controlled environment, you're able to develop a heightened awareness for when you lose focus.

You then build up to doing the "C-Grid" with a TV or your favorite music playing in the background. At first you'll get distracted by the TV or the beat of the music. Eventually you'll be able to lock in your focus and concentration so the voices and music fade into the background and you can feel yourself in the moment.

The following pages contain "C-Grids" that you can use. Some people will use pencil and go from the bottom left corner of each box to the top right so they can use the same sheet in the future by making an X, going from top left to the bottom right of each box in their second attempt. I have found that when you use a dry-erase marker or a sharpie and cross out the number completely, your time will improve because you will no longer be able to see the numbers you have crossed out. When you use a pencil or go from corner to corner, you will still be able to see and read the numbers you have crossed out, thus increasing your time. The main thing to remember is to be consistent so that you can keep track of your times and compare your results to help measure your progress.

Have fun with the "C-Grid." Compete against your best time and feel yourself developing the ability to focus in the present moment, on one thing at a time.

Keep track of your times on the next page.

Visit www.SoWhatNextPitch.com For

50 FREE Concentration Training Grids

CONCENTRATION GRID TIME TRACKER

Date/Time

____/____	____/____	____/____	____/____
____/____	____/____	____/____	____/____
____/____	____/____	____/____	____/____
____/____	____/____	____/____	____/____
____/____	____/____	____/____	____/____
____/____	____/____	____/____	____/____
____/____	____/____	____/____	____/____
____/____	____/____	____/____	____/____
____/____	____/____	____/____	____/____
____/____	____/____	____/____	____/____
____/____	____/____	____/____	____/____
____/____	____/____	____/____	____/____
____/____	____/____	____/____	____/____
____/____	____/____	____/____	____/____
____/____	____/____	____/____	____/____
____/____	____/____	____/____	____/____
____/____	____/____	____/____	____/____
____/____	____/____	____/____	____/____
____/____	____/____	____/____	____/____
____/____	____/____	____/____	____/____

Brian Cain Peak Performance, LLC
Concentration Training Grid
www.briancain.com
www.briancaininnercircle.com

64	12	20	15	69	80	31	57	95	61
71	63	05	73	07	36	38	91	83	58
39	01	53	42	62	35	43	04	59	89
34	78	09	70	97	72	24	87	88	40
44	47	67	27	85	41	16	77	74	84
54	55	76	93	92	10	98	48	45	00
33	66	46	49	21	75	94	18	52	14
81	82	06	28	68	08	23	60	11	99
02	03	86	37	25	30	26	50	22	17
51	79	13	65	56	96	90	29	32	19

Brian Cain Peak Performance, LLC
Concentration Training Grid
www.briancain.com
www.briancaininnercircle.com

64	12	20	15	69	80	31	57	95	61
71	63	05	73	07	36	38	91	83	58
39	01	53	42	62	35	43	04	59	89
34	78	09	70	97	72	24	87	88	40
44	47	67	27	85	41	16	77	74	84
54	55	76	93	92	10	98	48	45	00
33	66	46	49	21	75	94	18	52	14
81	82	06	28	68	08	23	60	11	99
02	03	86	37	25	30	26	50	22	17
51	79	13	65	56	96	90	29	32	19

Brian Cain Peak Performance, LLC
Concentration Training Grid
www.briancain.com
www.briancaininnercircle.com

64	12	20	15	69	80	31	57	95	61
71	63	05	73	07	36	38	91	83	58
39	01	53	42	62	35	43	04	59	89
34	78	09	70	97	72	24	87	88	40
44	47	67	27	85	41	16	77	74	84
54	55	76	93	92	10	98	48	45	00
33	66	46	49	21	75	94	18	52	14
81	82	06	28	68	08	23	60	11	99
02	03	86	37	25	30	26	50	22	17
51	79	13	65	56	96	90	29	32	19

Brian Cain Peak Performance, LLC
Concentration Training Grid
www.briancain.com
www.briancaininnercircle.com

64	12	20	15	69	80	31	57	95	61
71	63	05	73	07	36	38	91	83	58
39	01	53	42	62	35	43	04	59	89
34	78	09	70	97	72	24	87	88	40
44	47	67	27	85	41	16	77	74	84
54	55	76	93	92	10	98	48	45	00
33	66	46	49	21	75	94	18	52	14
81	82	06	28	68	08	23	60	11	99
02	03	86	37	25	30	26	50	22	17
51	79	13	65	56	96	90	29	32	19

Brian Cain Peak Performance, LLC
Concentration Training Grid
www.briancain.com
www.briancaininnercircle.com

64	12	20	15	69	80	31	57	95	61
71	63	05	73	07	36	38	91	83	58
39	01	53	42	62	35	43	04	59	89
34	78	09	70	97	72	24	87	88	40
44	47	67	27	85	41	16	77	74	84
54	55	76	93	92	10	98	48	45	00
33	66	46	49	21	75	94	18	52	14
81	82	06	28	68	08	23	60	11	99
02	03	86	37	25	30	26	50	22	17
51	79	13	65	56	96	90	29	32	19

Brian Cain Peak Performance, LLC
Concentration Training Grid
www.briancain.com
www.briancaininnercircle.com

64	12	20	15	69	80	31	57	95	61
71	63	05	73	07	36	38	91	83	58
39	01	53	42	62	35	43	04	59	89
34	78	09	70	97	72	24	87	88	40
44	47	67	27	85	41	16	77	74	84
54	55	76	93	92	10	98	48	45	00
33	66	46	49	21	75	94	18	52	14
81	82	06	28	68	08	23	60	11	99
02	03	86	37	25	30	26	50	22	17
51	79	13	65	56	96	90	29	32	19

Brian Cain Peak Performance, LLC
Concentration Training Grid
www.briancain.com
www.briancaininnercircle.com

64	12	20	15	69	80	31	57	95	61
71	63	05	73	07	36	38	91	83	58
39	01	53	42	62	35	43	04	59	89
34	78	09	70	97	72	24	87	88	40
44	47	67	27	85	41	16	77	74	84
54	55	76	93	92	10	98	48	45	00
33	66	46	49	21	75	94	18	52	14
81	82	06	28	68	08	23	60	11	99
02	03	86	37	25	30	26	50	22	17
51	79	13	65	56	96	90	29	32	19

Brian Cain Peak Performance, LLC
Concentration Training Grid
www.briancain.com
www.briancaininnercircle.com

64	12	20	15	69	80	31	57	95	61
71	63	05	73	07	36	38	91	83	58
39	01	53	42	62	35	43	04	59	89
34	78	09	70	97	72	24	87	88	40
44	47	67	27	85	41	16	77	74	84
54	55	76	93	92	10	98	48	45	00
33	66	46	49	21	75	94	18	52	14
81	82	06	28	68	08	23	60	11	99
02	03	86	37	25	30	26	50	22	17
51	79	13	65	56	96	90	29	32	19

Brian Cain Peak Performance, LLC
Concentration Training Grid
www.briancain.com
www.briancaininnercircle.com

64	12	20	15	69	80	31	57	95	61
71	63	05	73	07	36	38	91	83	58
39	01	53	42	62	35	43	04	59	89
34	78	09	70	97	72	24	87	88	40
44	47	67	27	85	41	16	77	74	84
54	55	76	93	92	10	98	48	45	00
33	66	46	49	21	75	94	18	52	14
81	82	06	28	68	08	23	60	11	99
02	03	86	37	25	30	26	50	22	17
51	79	13	65	56	96	90	29	32	19

Brian Cain Peak Performance, LLC
Concentration Training Grid
www.briancain.com
www.briancaininnercircle.com

64	12	20	15	69	80	31	57	95	61
71	63	05	73	07	36	38	91	83	58
39	01	53	42	62	35	43	04	59	89
34	78	09	70	97	72	24	87	88	40
44	47	67	27	85	41	16	77	74	84
54	55	76	93	92	10	98	48	45	00
33	66	46	49	21	75	94	18	52	14
81	82	06	28	68	08	23	60	11	99
02	03	86	37	25	30	26	50	22	17
51	79	13	65	56	96	90	29	32	19

Brian Cain Peak Performance, LLC
Concentration Training Grid
www.briancain.com
www.briancaininnercircle.com

64	12	20	15	69	80	31	57	95	61
71	63	05	73	07	36	38	91	83	58
39	01	53	42	62	35	43	04	59	89
34	78	09	70	97	72	24	87	88	40
44	47	67	27	85	41	16	77	74	84
54	55	76	93	92	10	98	48	45	00
33	66	46	49	21	75	94	18	52	14
81	82	06	28	68	08	23	60	11	99
02	03	86	37	25	30	26	50	22	17
51	79	13	65	56	96	90	29	32	19

Brian Cain Peak Performance, LLC
Concentration Training Grid
www.briancain.com
www.briancaininnercircle.com

64	12	20	15	69	80	31	57	95	61
71	63	05	73	07	36	38	91	83	58
39	01	53	42	62	35	43	04	59	89
34	78	09	70	97	72	24	87	88	40
44	47	67	27	85	41	16	77	74	84
54	55	76	93	92	10	98	48	45	00
33	66	46	49	21	75	94	18	52	14
81	82	06	28	68	08	23	60	11	99
02	03	86	37	25	30	26	50	22	17
51	79	13	65	56	96	90	29	32	19

Brian Cain Peak Performance, LLC
Concentration Training Grid
www.briancain.com
www.briancaininnercircle.com

64	12	20	15	69	80	31	57	95	61
71	63	05	73	07	36	38	91	83	58
39	01	53	42	62	35	43	04	59	89
34	78	09	70	97	72	24	87	88	40
44	47	67	27	85	41	16	77	74	84
54	55	76	93	92	10	98	48	45	00
33	66	46	49	21	75	94	18	52	14
81	82	06	28	68	08	23	60	11	99
02	03	86	37	25	30	26	50	22	17
51	79	13	65	56	96	90	29	32	19

Brian Cain Peak Performance, LLC
Concentration Training Grid
www.briancain.com
www.briancaininnercircle.com

64	12	20	15	69	80	31	57	95	61
71	63	05	73	07	36	38	91	83	58
39	01	53	42	62	35	43	04	59	89
34	78	09	70	97	72	24	87	88	40
44	47	67	27	85	41	16	77	74	84
54	55	76	93	92	10	98	48	45	00
33	66	46	49	21	75	94	18	52	14
81	82	06	28	68	08	23	60	11	99
02	03	86	37	25	30	26	50	22	17
51	79	13	65	56	96	90	29	32	19

Brian Cain Peak Performance, LLC
Concentration Training Grid
www.briancain.com
www.briancaininnercircle.com

64	12	20	15	69	80	31	57	95	61
71	63	05	73	07	36	38	91	83	58
39	01	53	42	62	35	43	04	59	89
34	78	09	70	97	72	24	87	88	40
44	47	67	27	85	41	16	77	74	84
54	55	76	93	92	10	98	48	45	00
33	66	46	49	21	75	94	18	52	14
81	82	06	28	68	08	23	60	11	99
02	03	86	37	25	30	26	50	22	17
51	79	13	65	56	96	90	29	32	19

Brian Cain Peak Performance, LLC
Concentration Training Grid
www.briancain.com
www.briancaininnercircle.com

64	12	20	15	69	80	31	57	95	61
71	63	05	73	07	36	38	91	83	58
39	01	53	42	62	35	43	04	59	89
34	78	09	70	97	72	24	87	88	40
44	47	67	27	85	41	16	77	74	84
54	55	76	93	92	10	98	48	45	00
33	66	46	49	21	75	94	18	52	14
81	82	06	28	68	08	23	60	11	99
02	03	86	37	25	30	26	50	22	17
51	79	13	65	56	96	90	29	32	19

Brian Cain Peak Performance, LLC

Concentration Training Grid
www.briancain.com
www.briancaininnercircle.com

64	12	20	15	69	80	31	57	95	61
71	63	05	73	07	36	38	91	83	58
39	01	53	42	62	35	43	04	59	89
34	78	09	70	97	72	24	87	88	40
44	47	67	27	85	41	16	77	74	84
54	55	76	93	92	10	98	48	45	00
33	66	46	49	21	75	94	18	52	14
81	82	06	28	68	08	23	60	11	99
02	03	86	37	25	30	26	50	22	17
51	79	13	65	56	96	90	29	32	19

Brian Cain Peak Performance, LLC

Concentration Training Grid
www.briancain.com
www.briancaininnercircle.com

64	12	20	15	69	80	31	57	95	61
71	63	05	73	07	36	38	91	83	58
39	01	53	42	62	35	43	04	59	89
34	78	09	70	97	72	24	87	88	40
44	47	67	27	85	41	16	77	74	84
54	55	76	93	92	10	98	48	45	00
33	66	46	49	21	75	94	18	52	14
81	82	06	28	68	08	23	60	11	99
02	03	86	37	25	30	26	50	22	17
51	79	13	65	56	96	90	29	32	19

Brian Cain Peak Performance, LLC
Concentration Training Grid
www.briancain.com
www.briancaininnercircle.com

64	12	20	15	69	80	31	57	95	61
71	63	05	73	07	36	38	91	83	58
39	01	53	42	62	35	43	04	59	89
34	78	09	70	97	72	24	87	88	40
44	47	67	27	85	41	16	77	74	84
54	55	76	93	92	10	98	48	45	00
33	66	46	49	21	75	94	18	52	14
81	82	06	28	68	08	23	60	11	99
02	03	86	37	25	30	26	50	22	17
51	79	13	65	56	96	90	29	32	19

Brian Cain Peak Performance, LLC
Concentration Training Grid
www.briancain.com
www.briancaininnercircle.com

64	12	20	15	69	80	31	57	95	61
71	63	05	73	07	36	38	91	83	58
39	01	53	42	62	35	43	04	59	89
34	78	09	70	97	72	24	87	88	40
44	47	67	27	85	41	16	77	74	84
54	55	76	93	92	10	98	48	45	00
33	66	46	49	21	75	94	18	52	14
81	82	06	28	68	08	23	60	11	99
02	03	86	37	25	30	26	50	22	17
51	79	13	65	56	96	90	29	32	19

Brian Cain Peak Performance, LLC
Concentration Training Grid
www.briancain.com
www.briancaininnercircle.com

64	12	20	15	69	80	31	57	95	61
71	63	05	73	07	36	38	91	83	58
39	01	53	42	62	35	43	04	59	89
34	78	09	70	97	72	24	87	88	40
44	47	67	27	85	41	16	77	74	84
54	55	76	93	92	10	98	48	45	00
33	66	46	49	21	75	94	18	52	14
81	82	06	28	68	08	23	60	11	99
02	03	86	37	25	30	26	50	22	17
51	79	13	65	56	96	90	29	32	19

Chapter 25 | WHO IS BRIAN CAIN?

About the Author

B rian M. Cain, MS, CMAA, is an expert in the area of Mental Conditioning, Peak Performance Coaching, and Applied Sport Psychology. He has worked with coaches, athletes, and teams at the Olympic level and in the National Football League (NFL), National Basketball Association (NBA), National Hockey League (NHL), Ultimate Fighting Championship (UFC), and Major League Baseball (MLB) on using mental conditioning to perform at their best when it means the most.

Cain has also worked with programs in some of the top college athletic departments around the country, including the University of Alabama, Auburn University, Florida State University, the University of Iowa, the University of Maryland, the University of Mississippi, Mississippi State University, Oregon State University, the University of Southern California, the University of Tennessee, Texas Christian University, Vanderbilt University, Washington State University, Yale University, and many others.

Cain has worked as a mental-conditioning consultant with numerous high school-, state-, and national-championship programs. He has delivered his award-winning seminars and presentations at coaches' clinics, leadership summits, and athletic directors' conventions all over the country. As a high-school athletic director, he is one of the youngest ever to receive the Certified Master Athletic Administration Certification from the National Interscholastic Athletic Administrators Association.

A highly sought-after Peak Performance Coach, clinician, and keynote and motivational speaker, Cain delivers his message with passion, enthusiasm, and in an engaging style that keeps his audiences entertained while being educated. Someone who lives what he teaches, Cain will inspire you and give you the tools necessary to get the most out of your career.

Find out when Cain will be coming to your area by visiting his calendar at **www.briancain.com**.

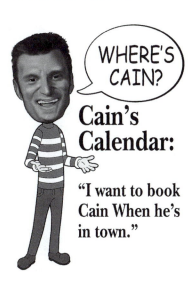

Chapter 26 | HOW YOU CAN BECOME A MASTER OF THE MENTAL GAME

Discover What The Inner Circle Delivers

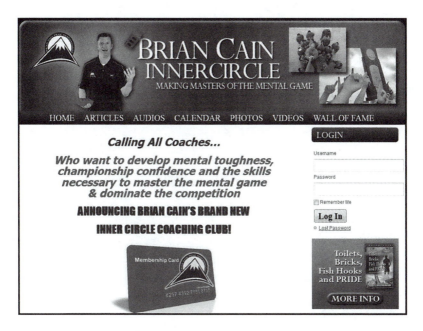

If you're a serious coach or athlete looking to take your performance to another level, I highly encourage you to join the Brian Cain Peak Performance Inner Circle. Lifetime members receive interviews with top coaches and athletes, videos of top performance routines, and inside access to Cain and his teachings. The Brian Cain Peak Performance Inner Circle will help you play at your best when it means the most. Log-on to **www.briancaininnercircle.com** to sign up today.

Chapter 27 | THE PEAK PERFORMANCE SYSTEM

PRIDE – Personal Responsibility In Daily Excellence

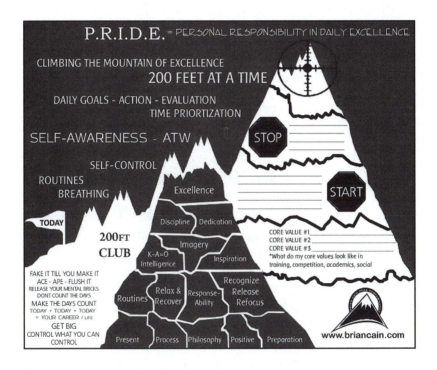

Have You or Your Team Ever Struggled With...

- Working hard physically *but still not getting the results you deserve?*

- Creating a system to *teach character and toughness* that translates to the field?

- *Investing time and money into books, videos and programs* that don't get results?

- Repeatedly *getting it done in practice, but failing to do so when the lights come on?*

- *Choking in pressure situations* time after time, even though you have been there before?

The Peak-Performance System Will...

- Give you the best step-by-step system for developing mental toughness ever created.

- Teach you the same mental-toughness system used by world-champion athletes.

- Be the equivalent of having the *world's best strength and conditioning coach... for your brain.*

- Positively *change your athletic and coaching career.*

- *Unlock your potential* and teach you how to be your best every day.

Cain's Peak Performance System (PRIDE – Personal Responsibility In Daily Excellence) is a six-DVD Peak Performance training program featuring eighteen 10-25 minute videos and a 100+ page manual designed for the coach or athlete looking to gain a competitive advantage from Peak-Performance and Mental-Toughness Training. Cain goes in-depth on the following topics:

1. The Language of Mental Toughness

2. 200FT Club & Core Covenants

3. Present-Moment Focus

4. Process-Over-Outcome Approaches

5. Championship Perspective

6. Positive Mental Attitudes

7. Preparation Routines for Confidence

8. Preparation Routines for Consistent Performance

9. RESPONSE-Ability Training

10. In-depth Relaxation & Recovery Training

11. Performance-Awareness Development

12. K-A=O – The Intelligence Factor

13. Mental-Imagery Training

14. Inspiration & Motivation that Works

15. Dedication & Commitment

16. Discipline as a Positive Life Skill

17. Excellence as a Lifestyle, Not an Event

18. Interview with An MMA World Champion

Visit www.briancain.com for more information

Visit http://youtu.be/aDaxlKLGTtw

**For A Sneak Peak of
The Peak Performance Bootcamp**

Chapter 28 | THE PEAK PERFORMANCE BOOTCAMP

Cain's Live Four Hour Seminar

2 DVD, 3 Audio CD, Manual

"Brian is a great presenter who has tremendous energy and had a very practical, use it today, method that coaches can use immediately."

John Tschida
University of St. Thomas

Learn the mental skills used by the best coaches and athletes in the World in Cain's 4-hour Peak Performance Bootcamp. Start performing at your best when it means the most and become a Master of The Mental Game.

Brian M. Cain, MS, CMAA is one of the top Peak Performance Coaches in the World today. Cain works with top professional, collegiate and high school coaches and athletes on becoming Masters of The Mental Game.

Learn more by visiting Cain online at www.briancain.com and sign up for his newsletter and free audio: The Top 10 Things World Champions Know That You Don't.

www.briancain.com
Approximate Program Time 4:03:24

BRIAN CAIN'S PEAK PERFORMANCE BOOTCAMP

BRIAN CAIN'S PEAK PERFORMANCE BOOTCAMP PROGRAM

BRIAN M. CAIN, MS, CMAA
Peak Performance Coach

BRIAN CAIN PEAK PERFORMANCE

Masters of The Mental Game Series Program

Have You or Your Team Ever Struggled With...

- The ability to *sustain consistent high levels of performance...*

- *Getting distracted* by a large crowd, hostile environment or "BIG GAME?"

- Finding ways to keep your team *motivated to work HARD & SMART everyday...*

- Ways to *make practice more competitive* and intense...

- *Choking in pressure situations* time after time even though you have been there before...

Today You Can Discover How To Help Your Team:

- Gain the mental toughness they need *out-play and out-perform* even the toughest competition...

- *Play in the moment* and destroy all those mental blocks that kill their performance...

- Take control over the speed and the flow of the game so all the competition is *playing at their pace*...

- Shatter their beliefs about what they "can't do"...

- Give them the tools *to accomplish things they once only dreamed of*...

- Develop the *team chemistry* you need to bring home a championship...

Visit www.briancain.com for more information

Visit http://youtu.be/_N3QxiYr2m4

For A Sneak Peak of The PRIDE Program In Action

By A College Baseball Program Committed To Excellence

Chapter 29 | INTRODUCTION TO PEAK PERFORMANCE AUDIO PROGRAM

Welcome to Mental Toughness Training

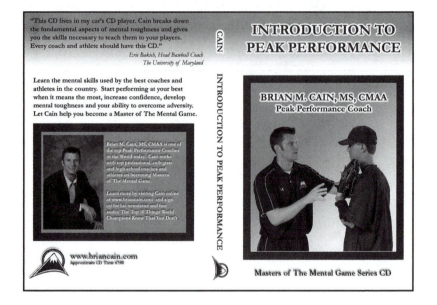

Have You or Your Team Ever Struggled With...

- Consistently *playing at your best...*

- Finding the motivation it takes to **work hard every day...**

- Maintaining **confidence** when you are *not playing well...*

- Choking in pressure situations **time after time** even though you have been there before...

The Introduction To Peak Performance CD Will...

- Give you insight into the *fundamentals of peak performance...*

- Help you to become a *Master of The Mental Game...*

- Increase your *ability to overcome adversity...*

- Teach you the psychological skills necessary to *perform consistently at your best...*

"This CD lives in my car's CD player. Cain breaks down the fundamentals aspects of mental toughness and gives you the skills necessary to teach toughness to your team. Every coach and athlete should have this CD in their car or on their IPOD at all times."

Eric Bakich
Head Baseball Coach
University of Maryland

At the elite levels, athletic performance is 90% mental and 10% physical.

In this CD you get the information you need to perform your best when it means the most.

You get the tactics, the training and the secrets you need to increase your mental toughness.

You get you the tools that will put your mental game MILES ahead of every other athlete and team in your league, in your conference or in your division.

That is exactly why I created this CD... so that YOU can discover:

- Why sport psychology and *peak performance is crucial* to your success this season!

- The tricks and methods that teach you how to *let go of the things you can't control* during play!

- The *3 "magic letters"* that turn statements of failure into goal-setting exclamations!

- How to make *excellence a LIFESTYLE* and not a once-in-a-while event!

- The little secrets that allow you to *increase your ability to play at a quicker tempo!*

- The right way – *and the wrong way – to talk on defense!*

"I started using this CD when I met Cain and it has helped me to be a better fighter, a better coach, more mentally tough and more confident. Learning to focus on the things I can control, learning that confidence is a choice, learning to not count the days but to make the days count has had tremendous impact on my career. Cain covers all of this and his P.R.I.D.E. program in this CD. I can't recommend this CD any more highly to the coach or athlete looking to increase their performance with mental toughness training."

Rob MacDonald
Professional Mixed Martial Arts Fighter, UFC
Strength and Conditioning Coach, Gym Jones

Visit www.briancain.com for more information

Chapter 30 | Toilets, Bricks, Fish Hooks and PRIDE

Cain's #1 Best Selling Book

Chapter 31 | CONNECT WITH CAIN
THROUGH SOCIAL MEDIA

Your Link to Doing a Little a Lot, Not a Lot a Little

Twitter = @briancainpeak
Facebook = Brian Cain Peak Performance
Linked In = Brian Cain Peak Performance
You Tube = wwwbriancaincom
ITUNES Podcast = Search Brian Cain

SIGN UP FOR YOUR FREE NEWSLETTER

www.briancain.com

Chapter 32 | PEAK PERFORMANCE & MENTAL CONDITIONING NOTES PAGES

Keeping It All In One Place

NOTES: _____

_____

_____

_____

_____

_____

_____

_____

_____

_____

_____

_____

_____

_____

_____

_____

_____

_____

_____

_____

_____

Brian Cain

Brian Cain

_____
_____
_____
_____
_____
_____
_____
_____
_____
_____
_____
_____
_____
_____
_____
_____
_____
_____
_____
_____
_____
_____
_____

_____
_____
_____
_____
_____
_____
_____
_____
_____
_____
_____
_____
_____
_____
_____
_____
_____
_____
_____
_____
_____
_____
_____
_____

_____

_____

_____

_____

_____

_____

_____

_____

_____

_____

_____

_____

_____

_____

_____

_____

_____

_____

_____

_____

_____

_____

_____
_____
_____
_____
_____
_____
_____
_____
_____
_____
_____
_____
_____
_____
_____
_____
_____
_____
_____
_____
_____
_____
_____
_____

_____

_____

_____

_____

_____

_____

_____

_____

_____

_____

_____

_____

_____

_____

_____

_____

_____

_____

_____

_____

_____

_____

_____

_____

_____
_____
_____
_____
_____
_____
_____
_____
_____
_____
_____
_____
_____
_____
_____
_____
_____
_____
_____
_____
_____
_____
_____
_____
_____
_____